Waging Peace

ANNE DEVESON spent her childhood in Malaya, Australia and England, but for most of her adult life she has lived in Sydney. She is a writer, documentary film-maker and former head of the Australian Film, Television and Radio School, with a long involvement in social justice.

Through her television and radio work, her books and articles, and her role with numerous organisations and boards, she has illuminated many social issues and influenced a wide range of policy. Her films have won three UN Peace awards and her books have been widely praised. They include the bestselling *Tell Me I'm Here*—about her son's struggles with schizophrenia—which won the 1992 Human Rights Award for non-fiction and was shortlisted in five major literary awards. Another bestseller, *Resilience*, weaves together research and reflection into a thought-provoking intellectual and personal story.

Anne was made an officer of the Order of Australia for her work in community health and for increasing public awareness of schizophrenia.

Anne Deveson has been the proud mother of three children, four stepchildren, three grandchildren, and a big gathering of step and step step grandchildren. She has a large yellow dog, four orange goldfish, a colourful garden and walls full of pictures and books. Her elder son Jonathan died in his early twenties, and still feels part of her family. She has many staunch and loving friends for whom she will always be grateful.

Waging Peace

Reflections on peace and war from an
unconventional woman

ANNE DEVESON

ALLEN&UNWIN
SYDNEY·MELBOURNE·AUCKLAND·LONDON

Published by Allen & Unwin in 2013

This project has been assisted by the Australian Government
through the Australia Council for the Arts, its arts funding
and advisory body.

Australian Government

Allen & Unwin
83 Alexander Street
Crows Nest NSW 2065
Australia
Phone: (61 2) 8425 0100
Email: info@allenandunwin.com
Web: www.allenandunwin.com

Cataloguing-in-Publication details are available
from the National Library of Australia
www.trove.nla.gov.au

ISBN 978 1 74331 003 8

Internal design by Emily O'Neill
Set in 12/17 pt Minion Pro by Bookhouse, Sydney
Printed and bound in Australia by Griffin Press

10 9 8 7 6 5 4 3 2 1

The paper in this book is FSC® certified.
FSC® promotes environmentally responsible,
socially beneficial and economically viable
management of the world's forests.

For my much loved grandchildren:
Bronte, Brodie and Odessa Blain

Live life generously, learn well, be kind

Contents

Wars and conflicts are not inevitable. They are caused by human beings. There are always interests that are furthered by war. Therefore those who have power and influence can also stop them.

Peace is a question of will. All conflicts can be settled, and there are no excuses for allowing them to become eternal. It is simply intolerable that violent conflicts defy resolution for decades causing immeasurable suffering, and preventing economic and social development . . . we should not accept any excuses from those in power.

Martti Ahtisaari, Nobel Peace Prize acceptance speech,
Oslo, 10 December 2008

Preface

From the beginning, this book became a journey that drew on history and memory as I asked the question, 'In a long life, what have I learned about peace?'

I grew up with war. War as a child in an English village, when German bombs began falling from the skies. War as my mother, brother and I fled England to join my father in Malaya, arriving not long before its invasion by the Japanese. War when my father was missing, believed killed, and we became refugees in Australia. And war when we were repatriated to a devastated England where we struggled to rebuild our lives.

I was fifteen years old, and war horrified me: the deaths of our closest friends, the devastation of London, the disappearance of my father, and the numbers of starving people sleeping rough on the streets. Looking back, I believe this is why I became a journalist. I needed to make sense of the world in which I lived. It's a story that begins in my childhood, winds its way through my life as a writer and film-maker—filming war in search of peace—and pursues my belief that, in spite of humanity's history of violence, there is an awakening of global accountability for keeping the peace, a shift in human consciousness that wasn't around when I was young.

Anne Deveson
January 2013

Encountering War

1

Growing Up with War

3 September 1939

A CHILD'S VIEW OF WAR

A day that comes back to me in small disturbing memories: the clatter of my mother's ivory cigarette holder falling to the floor; my brother John diving to retrieve it and making nervous jokes; my mother's fingers drumming on the table top; and all four of us gathered together, my mother, our nurse, my brother and I, gazing intently at the round black mouth of our wireless. For a moment, I think it might leap in the air and swallow me.

The wireless normally crouches on the dresser in among all the usual detritus of family life—old bus tickets and timetables, blunt pencils, broken pens, rubber bands and cough mixture.

My mother is still wearing the clothes in which she arrived. She'd heard a rumour that war might be declared and had travelled all night in a taxi from Edinburgh to our home in the south of England, fearing for our safety.

She lights a cigarette and tells us we must be quiet because the prime minister of England, Neville Chamberlain, is about to speak. She doesn't want to miss anything. His voice crackles through static—an old, tired voice, saying that the British government had given Germany until 11 am to withdraw their troops from Poland. No such undertaking had been received. Consequently Britain was at war with Germany.

'May God bless you all,' the prime minister says.

My mother lights another cigarette. 'I'd rather God saved us than blessed us.'

'But what's he saving us from?' I wail.

My brother grins. 'From being killed.'

I start chewing my hair. John is three years older than I am, and likes to tease me.

Outside, our garden is still serenely beautiful. Autumn leaves turning yellow, late-bloom pink roses, and apple trees heavy with fruit. My mother reaches out to hold our hands. 'We'll be all right.'

That night my brother entered my room and sat on my bed.

'War will mean eating nothing but bread and dripping,' he said with studied indifference.

'I like dripping,' I said smugly.

At that moment, a strong gust of wind tossed branches of a big pine tree against my bedroom window. The tree looked as if it wanted to come inside. I shivered, suddenly scared. I was nine years old, and I wanted the war to go away. All I knew was that we had dug an underground shelter in our back garden, put up blackout for our windows and tried on gasmasks that made us look like invaders from outer space. What I couldn't yet know was that this would be a war lasting almost six years and involving three-quarters of the world's population. Over 63 million people would die and many more would be injured.

The following morning, Nanny came into the kitchen with a copy of the day's newspaper. The headline was grim: BRITAIN AND FRANCE DECLARE WAR.

Nanny cleared her throat. 'I am going to join up, Moddom,' she said, turning red. 'I'm going into the navy, the Wrens.' This was the Women's Royal Naval Service, or WRNS.

My mother looked alarmed.

'You'll be all right, Moddom,' said Nanny, sounding slightly desperate. Nanny kept our household together. Her proper name was Mary Rusted but John and I didn't then know this. She wouldn't tell us her age. All she said was that she was sent out to work when she was twelve years old, as the youngest maid in an aristocratic household, where she was ordered to put her hair up and her skirts down. Her happiest memory was of being kissed by the pantry boy under the mistletoe on Christmas Eve when she was sixteen, and she'd never kissed anyone since.

—

Looking back, I suppose I had the conventional upbringing of a middle-class English child of that period, with a nanny who ruled the nursery, a brother who was sent to boarding school at the age of seven, and a father, Douglas, who was a rubber planter in Malaya (as it was known prior to independence in 1957 and federation in 1963 when the area was renamed Malaysia). That didn't mean he owned a rubber estate, but that he managed one for a large British company. A faded snapshot of my father shows a tall, good-looking man, dressed in immaculate knee-length white shorts, a white shirt and long white socks. He is holding me in his arms and looks awkward, which is hardly surprising because I have almost turned myself upside down.

My mother, Barbara, was the one who broke with convention. She was a successful fashion designer with her own business in London's West End, working largely for the burgeoning British film industry. She lived in London during the week, and returned to our house in Buckinghamshire most weekends, offering treats like breakfast together in bed and walks through the countryside, where she would allow us to get messy in ways that horrified our nurse.

Nanny had previously served the family of Admiral Evans, Lord Mountevans of the Broke, and came to us when I was two years old. She immediately decided that she had come down in the world. She had to put up with a family from the colonies—Malaya—furthermore, she was expected to wheel me around Kensington Gardens using an old white cane pram. 'Made in China,' she would snort, arms crossed. She insisted my mother go to Harrods and buy a large black carriage pram.

Then she started working on me. She coaxed me to stumble my way through at least part of the *Times* newspaper from the age of four because she had a passionate belief that gels needed just as good an education as boys. She also taught me numerous maxims, like: *Never a borrower nor a lender be, A stitch in time saves nine, Never leave a room empty-handed* and *The devil finds mischief for idle hands.*

In the kitchen the morning after war was declared, I ask if we can have a picnic lunch.

'It might be our last,' I wheedle.

Nanny plonks a bread board on the kitchen table and says, 'In that case, Moddom, I presume I'll be the one to arrange the picnic.'

My mother nods absent-mindedly. Nanny goes to her bedroom and returns wearing her best grey serge uniform and her hat with an enamelled badge of the Union Jack. We pack our picnic in a wicker basket and climb the hill to the little Norman church where every spring we pick primroses and bluebells from the woods that cradle the old stone building. Today, as a special treat, we have Playmate biscuits, iced with animal shapes in pink, white and chocolate.

'God Save the King,' says Nanny, waving her cup of tea. 'And God send Hitler to damnation.'

My brother and I wave our mugs of milk and solemnly chant, 'God Save the King.' And we giggle as we send Hitler to damnation.

'One must say Hitler is such a common little man,' we heard the vicar's wife declare at the village fete a few days later. It was autumn, and the conkers on the chestnut trees had already turned a handsome burnished brown. I was busy throwing them at cardboard cutouts of the common little man and missing every time, whereas my brother scored an instant bullseye just above Hitler's common little moustache.

War was simply too big to have a lot of meaning for me at nine or ten. Nanny gave us Union Jacks for our bedrooms, and we listened to songs like 'Run Rabbit Run' and 'We're Going to Hang Out the Washing on the Siegfried Line'. We had a wobbly old wind-up gramophone that made Vera Lynn sound drunk as she warbled '(There'll be Bluebirds Over) The White Cliffs of Dover'. Later, I reflected on the fact that those recordings early in the war carried mostly positive messages, unlike Eric Bogle's bitter and wonderful lament of the Vietnam War, 'And the Band Played Waltzing Matilda'.

We had no television to show us what was happening in other parts of the world, only stories about survivors of the First World War and how most of them had gone 'soft in the head', in Nanny's words. We knew that meant the loony bin.

Flags of the Union Jack began sprouting around gateways, growing out of chimney pots and in the village square. Red, white and blue bunting was draped around windows and doors. The post office handed out ration cards and everyone obediently queued. Posters mysteriously appeared on the walls of the post office, the railway station and outside the school. The one I remember most clearly showed men in khaki and helmets, grinning cheerily as they pointed at us: YOUR COUNTRY NEEDS YOU! I stared at it, bewildered. Why did my country need me? And what could I do?

Then there were the volunteer armies—or the Home Guard, as they were later called: men who were too old or infirm to join the regular army but who wished to help defend their country in the event of German invasion. By the end of July 1939, one and a half million men had volunteered. In the beginning they were poorly equipped and without funds or premises. They looked nervous and awkward in their stiff new khaki uniforms as they went door to door, inspecting blackouts and air-raid shelters, and making sure everyone had their gasmasks. Posters were everywhere:

HITLER WILL SEND NO WARNING
SO ALWAYS CARRY YOUR GASMASK

Gasmasks had to be collected from the church hall, including special tiny masks for babies. I remember thinking, 'But who would want to gas a baby?'

My mask was hot and horrible and made me gag when I fastened the straps around my neck. When I asked why we had to practise wearing them, my mother said that gas killed many soldiers and other people during the First World War and we had to make sure we weren't killed during the Second World War.

Blackouts had a similar defensive purpose. Before sunset, everybody had to cover their windows and doors with heavy blackout curtains, cardboard or paint. There could be no glimmer of light to aid enemy aircraft during their bombing raids. Streetlights were switched off or dimmed, and traffic lights and car headlights were fitted with special slotted covers to direct their beam downwards. Men were advised to leave their white shirt tails hanging out so they could be seen by drivers who had dimmed their headlights. Families were broken up as young women were sent to work on farms and in factories or to serve in the armed forces, and young men were ordered to the front lines to fight. Some never returned. This was when the postman began delivering bad news telegrams, and the sound of weeping spread through our village.

'They take the boys first,' said Nanny, who by now had received her papers to enlist with the Wrens. She was quickly promoted to petty officer cook, with dark blue braid on her smart new uniform and a whole cluster of young women under her command. For so many women who joined the services at that time, this was a first step towards some kind of emancipation, even though their pay was far less than men's.

But before this happened, two little boys from the East End of London were billeted with us, part of a mass evacuation of children from the larger cities that authorities felt certain would be bombed. Mothers accompanied very young children. Older children travelled alone, with luggage labels around their necks.

I remember our evacuees arriving. Their names were Jack and Dave, and they had never been to the countryside. I knew they were homesick because sometimes I would hear them crying at night. I'd tap on their bedroom door but they would tell me to go away.

Nanny gave them porridge for breakfast because she said they needed feeding up. They didn't like it. One Sunday evening when my mother went to play the piano, it gave a soggy moan. She opened the lid and looked down at a putrid, bubbling mass of grey. She sighed, then shrugged her shoulders. 'Far worse things are happening in the world.'

February 1940

MARCHING OFF TO WAR

Mists are rising milky grey over the marshes, wild ducks are flying, and the dairyman and his horse are delivering our rations as I leave for school, my gumboots squelching through the mud. It's Friday, when we sing not only the national anthem but also a hymn, because it is wartime and we have to support Our Majesty the King.

Eighty well-polished boys and girls, dressed in uniforms of brown and grey and chattering like sparrows, march into the church hall, led by an exasperated man with a megaphone who keeps telling us to swing our arms and keep our shoulders back. The megaphone man is our headmaster, Mr Stalin. His wife, Mrs Stalin, trots behind him, her left arm looped through the handles of a shiny black handbag.

'No relation of the Russian president,' Mrs Stalin explains hastily on her first meeting with my mother. Her Adam's apple bobs up and down and she turns bright red.

'I understand,' says my mother, attempting to sound kind.

When I first went to school I was six years old, and I sang lustily because I wanted to belong. When I was nine, I turned my attention to God, who worried me. He seemed to be responsible for just about everything that was happening in the world, including all creatures great and small—which included me, my brother, my parents, Nanny and our hamsters.

All things bright and beautiful,
All creatures great and small,
All things wise and wonderful:
The Lord God made them all.

So if the Lord God made us all, then why weren't we safe from harm? Why was God sending young men off to battle? Why did our hamsters die? Why did foxes kill chickens and chickens kill worms? No, no, it didn't make sense, I thought, squelching through the winter mud, my belief in the wisdom of God sinking into the mire.

—

Not long after war was declared, my mother took me to a paediatrician in London. Mrs Stalin had one morning whispered that she thought I just might have, perhaps not likely, but just possibly, curvature of the spine.

The Harley Street doctor looked at me and said, Rubbish, I was merely round-shouldered. 'Good job you're not a boy, young woman; you'd never make the army.'

'She's only nine,' snapped my mother.

Outside the cream prosperity of the doctor's consulting rooms, we turned in to Oxford Street and found a crowd of people waving red, white and blue streamers and cheering a straggle of soldiers in khaki uniforms who were marching down the road. The soldiers were young, their smiles were broad, their backs were straight. A brass band rumbled in their wake:

Onward, Christian soldiers,
Marching as to war,
With the cross of Jesus
Going on before.

This was the hymn I remembered as I stared at the soldiers, tapping my feet along with the band but feeling sick at the same time—a child who was afraid of bullies and thunderstorms, sensing that this wasn't a story with a happy ending, that many of these young men strutting out so tall and proud would be wounded or killed. At that moment, though, I wanted to be a hero, to march off to war with the soldiers. I wanted to act out the myths of Odysseus and Achilles with their shining swords and shields, their reckless quests for adventure. I wanted excitement. Yet I also felt so sad for these young men. Caught in the struggle between myth and reality, mind and heart warred with each other. I needed to cry at the same time as I wanted to cheer.

I picked up some streamers that lay near my feet and threw them in sprays of red, white and blue. I waved a flag. I took my mother's hand as she demanded exit and imperiously sliced her way through the crowds, trampling on a carpet of fallen copper leaves. Around the corner, she found us a cafe where we sat at a small round table with a white marble top. She ordered a hot chocolate for me and Earl Grey tea for herself. She stirred her tea carefully, even though it was black and without sugar, and I wondered why she was doing this, and why she was gazing so fixedly at the cup. When she ceased stirring, she put the teaspoon carefully on her saucer and looked up at me. Her eyes were filled with tears.

Some days later I was sitting at my desk when a wailing noise assailed my ears, getting louder and louder until I thought it might explode inside my head. It was an air-raid warning, much fiercer than any I had heard before. For a moment I didn't move but sat tracing the grain of wood on my desk, wondering why people wanted to kill each other and thinking how strange it was that bombs might suddenly drop from the sky.

Summer was long over, yet the thought flashed through my mind: would there ever be another summer? These were inchoate thoughts for a child who had little idea of the reality of war, but they reflected a growing realisation that real war was neither a game nor an exciting legend. Real war was terrible.

May–June 1940

HEROES AND OTHERS

After a series of rapid German victories over Denmark, Norway, Holland and Belgium, the war entered a new phase. One of my uncles, Kenneth—my mother's youngest and favourite brother—was a captain in the British navy. He was on leave towards the end of May 1940, by which time the German army had advanced almost to the French coast. Allied troops were being evacuated from the beaches of Dunkirk in a scramble of boats. Messerschmitt planes crisscrossed the sky like birds of prey while down below, in a cold grey sea, craft began sinking from the German bombardment; men leapt for safety, ducking machine-gun fire. All kinds of boats—fishing boats, tugs and trawlers, pleasure craft—tried to rescue them.

These were stupendously brave rescues by mostly British and local civilians, who risked their lives, hour after hour, crossing from one coast to another. My uncle and his partner were typical. They lived near the English seaside, and sailed across the Channel in their own small boat, picking up British and French survivors, taking them to safety, returning to Dunkirk for yet another load, tending to the wounded, nursing the dying. Yet afterwards, instead of being acclaimed, my uncle learned he was to be court-martialled. Someone had revealed his homosexuality to Naval Command. My uncle shot himself.

After her brother's death, my mother came down from London by train, arriving with her face swollen from crying.

She raged at the bigotry of a society that knew homosexuality existed but wouldn't allow it a public face. For most of that weekend she shut herself in her bedroom. Two cousins arrived, and hissed secrets over the kitchen table. I didn't understand what was happening, except that one minute my uncle had been a hero, and then suddenly he was in disgrace. A 'pervert', one of his fellow officers had said.

In my skein of memories, my uncle is still a bright strand with his wide smile, laughing eyes and a generosity of spirit that made me feel happy whenever he appeared. But even as a child I felt something had happened that was both horrible and unfair.

14 June 1940

DUTY TO GO

On this date, the German army marched into Paris, and France surrendered. Great Britain stood alone. By now, my father was in a state of panic, insisting we join him in Malaya. It wasn't an easy decision. By going, we were risking mines, U-boats and surface attacks from German planes and boats. By staying, we were exposing ourselves to German bombs, and possibly a German invasion. Telegrams sped between my father and my mother.

IMPERATIVE YOU BRING THE CHILDREN TO SAFETY
LOVE DOUGLAS

At first, my mother resisted my father's messages. Then, one day, Nanny—who by now was in the Wrens—came for a visit. She was red-faced and indignant as she settled herself firmly in a kitchen chair.

'Moddom, for your children's sake, it is your duty to go.'

2

Journey

22 July 1940

DECK QUOITS AND DEPTH CHARGES

The voyage is long. We are on a huge passenger liner, the *Viceroy of India*, sailing in the middle of a troop convoy of ships, heading for Malaya.

The night we boarded the ship, anxious crowds were gathered everywhere we looked. People cried as they leaned over the ship's railings, shouting their goodbyes. Streamers of every colour waved in a limp grey sky. A brass band on shore played 'Rule Britannia' as we stared into the distant throng of weepers. I was looking for Nanny. I waved back until my hands began to ache, and I remember wondering if we would ever see her again. And then I found her: Nanny in her smart blue uniform, hoping we would notice her as she waved goodbye.

The *Viceroy of India* had been one of the last grand P&O passenger liners—vintage 1930s—until the war came and she was converted into a troop carrier. She was still elegantly designed and beautifully appointed, with two theatres, an indoor swimming pool, woodwork of mahogany and pine, and cabins with extra rooms for servants. But now all cabins had been vastly reduced in size to take as many passengers as possible. Ours seemed scarcely large enough for a family of snails, but we were too tired to care. John had the top bunk, our mother a bed of her own, and I wriggled into the bottom bunk, complaining loudly.

I lay in the darkness thinking about my father and whether I would recognise him. I tried to imagine what might happen if we were sunk by a German U-boat. Eventually, I drifted off to sleep. Later, I woke to the thrumming of the ship's engines and my brother tugging at me to go on deck. I held John's hand as we watched the sea hurtling towards us. We were on an adventure taking us from one side of the world to another—but to what? What would we find?

My head thrummed with memories and emotions: our home in England, Nanny and our old life; our father—almost a stranger—and our mother and our new life. What would it be like?

'It'll be fun,' said my brother.

I nodded. At the moment, it didn't feel like fun.

Far out into the Atlantic Ocean we sailed, through grey seas and gusty winds. Our ship was accompanied by three other passenger liners, and protected by two escort ships, HMS *Vanquisher* and HMS *Westcott*, much smaller ships that always seemed to be in a hurry.

'Good job they're there,' said John. 'They're to protect us from U-boats.'

—

As weeks at sea enfolded us, and the weather grew warmer, I ceased worrying. Phosphorus gleamed around the bows of our ship, dolphins played and a giant albatross wheeled overhead.

Ever confident of his knowledge, my brother pulled at my arm and pointed to the albatross. 'They can live for fifty years or more, and it's bad luck to kill them, because people believe they are the souls of lost sailors.'

He quoted Coleridge's 'Rime of the Ancient Mariner':

It is an ancient Mariner,
And he stoppeth one of three.
'By thy long grey beard and glittering eye,
Now wherefore stopp'st thou me? . . .'

When he became bored with the Ancient Mariner, my brother tried to scare me into believing the world was going to end. I paid him back by giving him a glass of Epsom salts and telling him it was lemonade.

We probably squabbled because deck games and splashing in the pool had given way to the priority of life jackets and lifeboat drill. Rumours flew down the ship's claustrophobic corridors that German submarines had sunk a vessel in our convoy. Then it became two vessels, then three, and finally the submarines were said to be heading our way. My brother said I should learn to swim.

On the afternoon of 11 August, our ship's speed increased noticeably. News spread that we were steaming to the aid of a British ship that was sinking fast. Two other vessels came into sight. One was a warship, the other a liner. As we approached we could see a great hole in the liner's side.

'As big as two London buses,' said John, as we hung over the rails of the deck. Surely this must have been the work of a German submarine, rather than a collision with another ship as we'd been told.

'Must have been a hefty collision,' said my brother, looking down at the gaping hole in disbelief.

The sea was tossing lifeboats as if they were wooden toys. The boats were crammed with passengers, white-faced from seasickness, shock and cold. After that, there were nights when I would lie awake, gripping the sides of my bunk, believing that I could hear a submarine scraping alongside. Soon the porthole would crack and the sea come rushing in. I wondered how long I could hold my breath.

Yet between nights of fearful anticipation there were deck quoits and competitions. Ice-cream at 11 am—chocolate, pink and vanilla, with wafers—served on deck. Our mother sunning herself in a deck chair and the smell of suntan oil. Notices delivered under cabin doors: NO BOISTEROUS GAMES ON THE SABBATH.

Our journey was coming to an end. My brother had at last taught me to swim. I had made friends with other children on the ship. But I was anxious about my father. I hoped he would realise that I was no longer a child; that I was ten years old and growing up fast—too fast, as I found to my cost when we reached Penang.

3

Malaya

5 September 1940

NEW LIVES IN MALAYA

When we finally docked in Penang, the air was warm and sultry. My father was waiting to greet us on the dockside, a tall stranger in shorts and long white socks, smoking a pipe and pacing up and down. He kissed my mother, shook my brother's hand, and patted me on the head. I tried to jump into his arms, forgetting how much I had grown. As I leapt, I knocked his pipe out of his hand. It rolled into the murky water of Penang Harbour. He winced. I blushed.

'You behaved like an idjit,' my brother summed it up later.

I was disappointed and angry. For a long time it seemed that no matter how hard my father and I tried, we were always awkward with one another—as if we were running a three-legged race, tied together but pulling in opposite directions.

—

I liked our house in Malaya. It was a big wooden bungalow with a palm-thatched roof which housed lizards, insects and a nest of baby owls. I enjoyed racing up and down the wide verandahs, and visiting the cookhouse that smelled of incense and spices and tropical fruits. Dark groves of rubber trees flanked two sides of our property, the jungle loomed tall and mysterious on the other two sides; and yes, said my father, tigers were there, and monkeys and snakes. Our house wasn't far from an old valley town called Kuala Pilah, with many old Chinese shophouses fronting the main street, and a marketplace we went to for treats.

At night my parents played records on a wind-up gramophone, and sometimes they danced. Their favourite song was 'Plaisir d'amour'. Occasionally I hung around, hoping my father would kiss my mother, but it never happened while I was present. I have a sepia photograph of my mother and father from this time, wearing fancy dress for a New Year's Eve party. My father wears a false red nose and my mother a Japanese kimono. All the guests look innocently happy, unaware of how soon their lives would be so cruelly changed.

We had only just settled in to our new lives in Malaya when my father announced that he wanted to send me to a convent boarding school in the Cameron Highlands—one of the few schools considered suitable for the daughters of English gentlemen. No schools were considered suitable for the sons of English gentlemen, so my brother stayed at home and was given a tutor. This seemed unfair to me, as did the way Chinese and Malay staff called my brother Tuan Kechil, literally 'Little Lord', while I was known as Missee, or 'Little Miss'.

I hated boarding school. The nuns' robes frightened me, especially at night when they looked like large black bats, flitting between rows of dormitory beds. This was the first time I had slept away from home, so I missed my mother, and I was considered so untidy I had to keep the contents of my desk in a garbage bin which was inspected at regular intervals in front of the entire school. Tears of homesickness resulted in spending three hours alone in the chapel, praying to Jesus or the Virgin Mary. I decided to throw in my lot with the Virgin Mary.

I had only been at the school for one term when my life changed again. My father believed Japan might enter the war on Germany's side and he brought me home. Rumours were gathering among the villagers of imminent invasion. 'Send the children away,' implored the Japanese laundrywoman, tugging at my father's sleeve. 'Japanese come. Many soldiers. Many planes. Bring war. Send children away.'

At the end of 1941, my parents flew with us to the safety of Perth, in Western Australia, where they settled us into Australian boarding schools before they returned to Malaya.

This time my father did hug me. 'Take care, old girl,' he said. And then he turned to my brother. 'Look after your sister, there's a good chap.'

December 1941

JAPANESE ON BICYCLES

My father's reactions to the threat of war weren't based solely on rumours. He read widely and was intensely interested in Britain's colonial history and its role in the East. From the moment he arrived in Malaya he had tried to learn about Malay, Chinese, Japanese and Indian cultures. He had many

Asian friends. And he openly criticised the widespread British practice at that time of treating Asian people as if they were inferior, which included banning them from European clubs, no matter how high their professional status.

'One day we'll pay for this,' he wrote in one of his diaries. 'We take over their country, show no respect for their culture or their lives, and persist in behaving as if we were the superior race.' He didn't believe that Japan would be the pushover that most British people seemed to think. He disliked racism and rejected jokes that the Japanese were 'monkey men' with their baggy uniforms and sandshoes, or that they were half blind and had to set off firecrackers so they could see.

He also observed that all Malaya's defences were directed seawards, yet there was nothing to stop invaders coming by land. Most British leaders dismissed this idea. Yet this was how the Japanese army advanced. Riding ordinary old bicycles they invaded the Malay Peninsula, rifles slung over their shoulders, moving swiftly and silently, whereas the British and Australian soldiers, wearing boots and heavy uniforms, were slow and ill-equipped for jungle fighting.

My father would have been even more disturbed had he known that, in the autumn of 1940, the British War Cabinet's thinking on the defence of Malaya had secretly undergone a critical change. Prime Minister Winston Churchill had surreptitiously overruled an earlier decision that placed Malaya second in defence importance to the British Isles. Now, due to heavy military losses in Europe, Malaya was ranked below the Middle East and Russia.

Churchill's next decision was to abandon defence of the whole of Malaya and instead concentrate only on Singapore.

He ignored the fact that in Singapore there were no tanks, too few guns and any remaining planes were obsolete. It was as if the British military refused to believe that Fortress Singapore, the pride of the British Empire, could ever fall to the 'inferior' Japanese. They were wrong.

In the early hours of 7 December 1941, the Japanese launched a devastating surprise attack against the United States naval base at Pearl Harbor in Hawaii, killing 2402 Americans and wounding 1282. The United States immediately declared war on Japan, and Australia followed suit. An hour earlier, the Japanese offensive had begun with landings in Malaya at Kota Bharu on the north-east coast and in Thailand, while bombing raids destroyed British aerodromes and planes in the north. Kota Bharu was the first major battle of the Pacific War.

Singapore also received its first heavy raid, at 4 am on 8 December 1941, assisted by the lights of party-goers who obligingly illuminated the city as they danced their lives away.

Two days later, Japanese aircraft bombed and sank the battleship *Prince of Wales* and the cruiser *Repulse*. Both ships had been sent to reinforce Malaya's defences; 840 men died.

Winston Churchill was profoundly shocked by news of the sinkings. In his war diary, he wrote: 'As I turned over and twisted in bed the full horror of the news sank in upon me . . . Over this vast expanse of waters, Japan was supreme.'

In Malaya, the disasters continued. On the morning of 11 December, Japanese aircraft swooped over Penang and reduced it to flames and rubble. At least a thousand bodies were buried under the debris.

The speed and success of the Japanese advances took everyone by surprise. Only four days earlier, Sir Shenton

Thomas, the last governor of the Straits Settlements with their capital Singapore, had told his cipher clerk, 'You can take it from me, there will never be a Japanese bomb dropped in Singapore, there will never be a Japanese set foot in Malaya.'

—

In Malaya and Australia, the loss of the *Prince of Wales* and the *Repulse* had a terrible impact on morale. One of my classmates overheard a workman at the school say, 'The Japs will take us over. You wait and see.' This notion terrified us, and when a favourite teacher asked me if everything was all right, I didn't know how to answer. How could I know? I'd begun biting my fingernails and my schoolwork was suffering. Sometimes I would hang around the staffroom to see if I could borrow a newspaper. One of the older teachers told me I was too young to read all that stuff about war. I looked at her in amazement. 'But I need to read it. I need to know.'

I had nightmares about my parents being killed by the Japanese. My brother said he had no dreams. He forbade them to enter his mind.

As the Japanese advanced from the north-west coast, thousands of Malay and Chinese citizens fled south by any means possible. But none were allowed to take public transport or clog the roads until the European population had been evacuated. Governments ordered ex-pats to pack up and leave without a word to their Asian staff, who felt deeply betrayed. Volunteer defence forces were obliged to hand over their weapons to the regular army, and their local knowledge and skills were rarely called upon. Likewise, few attempts were made to harness the willing support of Malay and Chinese locals. On 16 December 1941 an editorial in the *Malayan Gazette* read:

> People in Penang are still stunned by the sudden invasion of the Japanese and still shocked by the desertion of the British. Has Britain really deserted us? Then why have her troops been evacuated from the island—to leave us to fend for ourselves? We still cannot get over the dismay of Britain failing us in our hour of need. Why has Britain failed? How can she fail? The great invincible Empire fail? Is it possible? . . . Our hopes, dreams and even our lives are in her hands. Has she really let us down?

Many felt that the malaise in Malaya was deep-rooted. At its heart was an aversion to treating members of the Asian races on a basis of equality. 'Allies with our servants and cooks . . . our tailors and our sewage coolies, may Heaven forbid!' said a British army volunteer when he spoke to Ian Morrison, the London *Times* correspondent, about the failure of the different racial communities to work together.

By law the Malays were sovereign over Malaya but, effectively, Malaya was governed by the British. 'The British and the Asiatics live their lives apart . . . and the small British community forms no more than a thin and brittle veneer,' wrote Morrison. 'No uniting force bound the community together.'

The battle for mainland Malaya was over by 1 February 1942. Over 30,000 British troops, who had been fighting on the mainland, had crossed the causeway that linked the straits of Jahore to Singapore Island. The last to come were 250 men of the Argyll, marching to their bagpipes, heads held high.

I wondered, if I were a soldier, would I hold my head high? Held high, it might be easier to blow it off. These were macabre thoughts for an eleven-year-old—but for me, macabre thoughts were one way of confronting terror.

With the Japanese invasion of Malaya, Australia and the United States had acquired a common enemy. It was imperative for both countries to prevent Japan from taking control of the South Pacific and interrupting American supply lines. America agreed to help Australia because Australia was the ideal base from which to launch a US attack on Japan—and Australian prime minister John Curtin knew that without an American presence, Australia was unprotected in the face of a Japanese invasion. Curtin delivered his New Year's message to the Australian people in an article published in the Melbourne *Herald* of 27 December 1941:

> I make it quite clear that Australia looks to America, free of any pangs as to our traditional links or kinship with the United Kingdom. We shall exert all our energies to shaping a defence plan, with the US as its keystone, which will enable us to hold out until the tide swings against the enemy.

This was brave and radical thinking. It had repercussions throughout the whole of South-East Asia, and signalled the ending of British sovereignty in the Far East. It also strained Australia's relationship with Great Britain. Curtin was insistent that Australian soldiers fighting in the Middle East be returned to defend Australia from the steadily advancing Japanese. He was outraged that Churchill had already diverted one division towards Burma without first seeking his approval. Top-secret cables flashed between the two leaders until Churchill reluctantly agreed to return the Australian troops.

Curtin also understood the cost of Britain's inability to defend Malaya. AN INEXCUSABLE BETRAYAL, was the message he sent in a cablegram to Churchill.

'It's very serious, Anne,' my brother John told me, wiping his glasses. 'A lot of things are going to change.'

John was right. The fall of Singapore marked a pivotal moment in Australia's history. It signalled the effective end of British imperial power in Asia and the eventual emergence of Asian nationhood. It irrevocably altered Australian ties with Britain and placed us on the path to independence.

Meantime, Singapore partied. Margaret Shennan's book *Out in the Midday Sun* describes how a bemused officer who was stationed in Singapore with other Australian troops viewed the formal mess dress and finery of the British in wartime Singapore: 'Either we were crazy or they were crazy. Either there was danger, or there was no danger.'

13 February 1942

THE FALL OF SINGAPORE

Singapore was on fire. Thousands of civilians—men, women and children—were waiting to embark on any ship that might come to their rescue. Japanese planes roared overhead, blowing up ships and boats as they tried to make their escape. Some 3000 people died at sea. Two days later, on 15 February, Singapore surrendered.

John Curtin's press statement declared: 'The fall of Singapore can only be described as Australia's Dunkirk. . . . Our honeymoon has finished. It is now work or fight as we have never worked or fought before.'

4

Becoming Refugees

19 February 1942

DARWIN BOMBED

Four days after the fall of Singapore, Darwin was bombed. Two waves of planes swept across the Australian sky, killing 243 people and injuring several hundred more. Darwin was completely unprepared. Its young soldiers were untrained; fuses on their guns were damaged and didn't work; their shells were the wrong kind. 'It was a big shemozzle,' one frail veteran told me when I visited Darwin some seventy years later. The old man had been a twenty-year-old gunner in 1942.

A series of Japanese air raids on Broome and Wyndham in Western Australia, and further attacks on Darwin, shocked the country. My brother and I, safe in Perth, were frantic for news of our parents.

My mother had written to my brother, saying everyone she knew had fled south to Singapore. Our father was fighting with a volunteer civilian army in the jungle, while she was sleeping alone in our bungalow with a Malay sword under her pillow.

When John received her letter, he acted swiftly. He arrived at my school, red-faced from running, and hid in the bushes until I and my classmates appeared for our morning tea (a soggy bun that for some reason was known as an 'orderly'). John had decided that we should run away from school for the rest of the day and call upon one of our parents' friends, who he was sure would give us more than the scant information we had been able to glean from our teachers. To feed ourselves, we filled a dormitory pillowcase with plums we stole from an orchard. The plums stained the pillowcase red. It occurred to me that this was how my parents' blood would look if Japanese soldiers killed them. I started to cry.

'It's all right,' said my brother, hugging me. 'They'll be fine.'

'How d'you know they'll be fine?'

'Because I know,' he said, and wiped my tears with a plum-stained handkerchief.

My brother was right about our parents, although there were weeks when we thought our father was dead. As for our mother, when the fighting drew so near that she could hear the guns, she grabbed our dog, Liza, and drove down to Singapore, just ahead of the Japanese soldiers riding their bicycles. From Singapore, she managed to escape to Darwin on one of the last planes flying to Australia. She arrived with almost no money, no passport and nowhere to stay. Her one bag contained beach sandals, a towel, a shirt and a pair of bathers, all she had been able to grab.

The city was in chaos, with long queues of people waiting for planes. She worked at a Darwin pub, making rice salads with glacé cherries and canned tuna fish, until she had the fare for a flight to Perth, where we had a tumultuous meeting at the airport. Then we went straight to the Cottesloe boarding house where we had stayed when we first came to Perth to find schools a few months earlier. Our mother had arranged with the owner, Mrs Cusworth, to care for us during weekends and holidays. I think she felt that visiting Mrs Cusworth would be more fun for us than being full-time boarders at school.

Mrs Cusworth was the archetypal housekeeper/grandmother whose arms were always open wide for cuddles and laughter. She wore old-fashioned lace-up corsets—one pink and one white—which we often spotted on the clothesline. Three or four times a week, she'd make us Yorkshire puddings dripping with gravy, even if we were in the middle of a heat wave. Then she'd tell us stories about death from botulism. 'Bottled fruit can give you botulism any time,' she said cheerfully, as she served us bottled plums, pears, apricots and peaches.

Mrs Cusworth was also looking after two other families. They were longstanding friends of my parents, and the wives had coincidentally met up with each other while seeking news of their husbands from the Red Cross. Together we made up a defiant little group of three mothers and five children, all dependent on the Red Cross for support. As well as Mrs Cusworth, our household consisted of my mother, John and I (our father was missing); our friend and honorary aunt Doreen Gore, who was already very ill with a tropical disease called sprue, and her two children, Peta and Jimmy (their father, Ginger, my father's best friend, was possibly a prisoner in Changi camp in Singapore); and Juliet James, known as Yette, and her daughter Judy (Yette's husband, Jimmy James, was missing, presumed dead).

Every morning, our mothers would go to the dockside hoping that their husbands might arrive on one of the last boats from Singapore to reach safety. Every morning our mothers would return looking so sad that sometimes we felt our roles as parents and children were reversed.

One day, as our mothers pushed open Mrs Cusworth's garden gate, we knew just by looking at them that the news was bad. 'No more men are escaping,' said my mother in a flat voice. 'Not likely, that's what they said.'

I don't remember how any of us filled the rest of the day. I think I read, went for a walk, and cried. The two boys chucked stones along the length of the beach. Our mothers probably drank endless cups of tea, or else raided their one communal bottle of gin: 'Mother's ruin,' they called it.

March 1942

REFUGEES ON THE LAND

Because we had no money, a cheerful, well-organised woman from the Red Cross in Perth sent us to live on a run-down property in Armadale, an hour's drive from the city.

'You could live off the land,' said the Red Cross woman, smiling brightly.

The farmhouse was a dilapidated old building with verandahs extending on three sides. A few straggly grey-green eucalypts bordered the dirt driveway, and at the back, just outside the sagging fly-screen door of the kitchen, was a huge fig tree. The first time we saw the tree we rushed to climb it, whooping with delight, but the figs were dry and disappointing.

With my penchant for melodrama, I decided this was a place of desolation and we were the wreckage. I would stand on the verandah, kicking the base of one of the posts, wanting to get away, wanting something . . . anything . . . to happen.

There was a drought. The soil that had supported generations of battlers was tired. Our mothers had been used to all the comforts of a colonial life, so they barely knew how to boil an egg, let alone milk a cow. The first time they did the washing, they used so much starch the sheets flapped like plasterboard from the sagging clothesline and had to be washed again.

The property in Armadale was owned by an ear, nose and throat specialist who had bought it for his retirement. He was a pompous old man in his seventies, who wore an ancient Panama hat and a gold fob chain dangling from his corpulent middle. He had a harelip, which made him difficult to understand. Only when I was an adult did I see any irony in his affliction. The property came with an odd-job man called Rose. Old Man Rose was employed by Dr Jewett to look after his land and his dwindling cattle, which were dominated by a large black and white bull. As we discovered, Old Man Rose spent most of his time drinking in the hayloft, and the hours of his day were measured by empty beer bottles scattered on the concrete floor at the foot of the haystack.

Dr Jewett was equally memorable. He never let us forget that allowing us to live on his property was his contribution to the war effort. Every Sunday he would churn up the dusty driveway in an old blue Holden and begin a tour of inspection, poking at the weeds that choked the flowerbeds, banging the rusty water tanks with his cane—grumbling because they were nearly empty, as if it were our fault it hadn't rained—and thumping into the kitchen with its cracked grey linoleum and broken windows.

'How's the stove?' he'd whistle through his moist yellowing moustache, pointing to the old green and cream Kooka stove that was caked with generations of blackened food. He would test the mantelpiece for dust by wiping his finger along a row of bronze and silver sports trophies, chipped and discoloured. The last part of this routine was to tell our mothers how to make tea. 'You bring the kettle to the pot, not the pot to the kettle,' he would say. The pot always took hours to boil and the tea was never strong enough for his satisfaction.

In between his noisy slurps, he would deliver a tirade about the decline and fall of the British Empire which, he said, served the English right because of their high-falutin' ways. Australia was God's own country and the Poms were finished. Jewett was a thin man, made fat by his self-importance, and we hated him, but I can see he was obviously nonplussed by the presence of these women with their brood of rebellious children who mimicked his speech and turned his oil paintings of fly-blown hollyhocks and stags at bay to face the wall.

On one particular day, after we had rolled our eyes at his departing car, our mothers corralled us into the strawberry patch that was supposed to provide fruit we could sell. But the few strawberries that had survived the long hot summer were brown and shrivelled.

As the morning lengthened, the heat became intense. Suddenly, gentle white-haired Aunt Doreen said miserably, 'It's no good, Bea—there's nothing worth picking.'

. My mother wiped her hands on her shirt. Sweat trickled down her neck. She looked defiant. 'They're not all bad.'

'Yes, they are,' we children shouted.

'They're not.'

'They are.'

We'd gone too far. She rushed at us, shouting angrily as we scattered in all directions. But then I stopped, even though I could outrun her. Until then, she had been simply our mother—quick to praise us, fierce in our defence. She corrected our manners and manifested harmless English snobberies—like insisting we said *lavatory* not *toilet*—which deeply embarrassed my brother and me. Occasionally she would lose her temper, but we knew when to get out of her way.

Now I stood transfixed by this woman in her scarlet shirt, her hair falling out of its roll at the nape of her neck. For a second I thought she might hit me, but she just stood there, panting. I realised her anger wasn't directed at us but at our circumstances, and that whatever happened, she wasn't going to be beaten. As I watched she shrugged, smiled wryly, and walked away.

Whenever I am under siege I can still catch a glimpse of her pounding over that paddock, red shirt, black rubber shoes, feet splayed; it's not so much an image of her as a reminder to keep going—forward not back. Jung wrote that every mother carries her daughter in herself and every daughter her mother, and every woman extends backwards into her mother and forward into her daughter. I would like to think that when my mother made her celebrated charge across the paddock, brandishing her hoe, she anointed me with the order of resilience. Resilience was perhaps her greatest quality, one that came to interest me deeply, so that many years later I wrote a book about it, simply entitled *Resilience*.

Days passed in clouds of dry red dust. Sometimes we walked down to the village and on the way gathered mushrooms which we took to the local store to sell. Our mothers were too exhausted to know what we were doing. We kept out of their way and managed to convince them we were schooling ourselves in the hayloft. We had tried going to the village school by harnessing an old horse to an even older sulky, but the horse bolted, throwing us into a ditch by the side of the road. So we drew up a timetable, which we hoped would impress our mothers and stop any further questions. English consisted of reading books like *Lady Chatterley's Lover*, which we had found in a box of books in the laundry. Nature study involved organising races between grasshoppers or other unfortunate insects. Biology entailed giggling as we cautiously explored our bodies—boys not allowed.

Looking back, this wasn't a happy time. We were poor. Food was scarce. Doreen remained ill, and medicine was expensive. But the worst part was that even though we were safe, the lack of news about our missing fathers and husbands hovered night and day, so war never left us. I wanted my father with his pipe, his poems, and even his grumpy moods.

My mother Barbara Deveson,
my brother John and me,
around 1931 in Malaya.

My father Douglas Deveson,
around 1932 in Malaya.

Me and John in London, 1934.

Me, my mother and John out
on the town in London, 1935.

Patsy and me at Cottesloe Beach in Western Australia, 1941.

My mother and me in Hay Street, Perth, 1941.

My father, me and John back in the United Kingdom after the war, Derbyshire, 1948.

Ellis and me in Hobart, 1959.

5

Escaped

Perth, February 1943

ENDINGS AND NEW STARTS

One afternoon, four of us children were hoeing the strawberry patch in a desultory fashion when we heard a roar that sounded as if the bull had escaped. We knew that my brother was in the lower paddock so we rushed down the hill towards him, when around a bend in the dusty road came a taxi. A man's elbow was sticking out of one of the windows. It was my father's! He was dazed and shaky as he climbed out of the taxi, and so thin I was scared he might fall down.

Everyone ran out. Mothers and children hugging, shouting, jumping up and down. Somewhere in the middle of this tumult of joy I heard Doreen and Yette asking tremulously about their own husbands, and my father saying, 'I'm sorry, I'm so sorry. I tried to find them, I tried . . .' He cried in great gulping sobs, his chest heaving as my mother held one hand and Yette the other. He was shivering and had a fever. I had never seen my father cry and I wanted to run and hug him, but I was scared he would push me away. I watched him from the doorway, tears in my eyes.

He was suffering from a severe attack of malaria. The following morning, a Red Cross car took him back to the hospital in Perth, where he stayed for two or three weeks. My mother went down to see him and said he must be getting better: he was beginning to grumble.

It was two or three weeks before he'd tell us what had happened to him in the last few days before Singapore surrendered to the Japanese. He had joined up with a police rescue squad, working to pull people from burning buildings. The whole dockside was ablaze. On the dockside he bumped into a young English sailor—Dick—whom he'd helped escape earlier that day. Dick told my father that he and a few other men had found a launch the British navy was meant to have scuttled, but they hadn't done the job properly.

'We're going to fix it and try to get to Sumatra,' said Dick, automatically ducking as gunfire whistled over his head. 'D'you want to make a getaway with us, guv?'

My father hesitated. He was not normally prone to making quick decisions.

'Go on,' encouraged Dick, 'or I'll have to find someone else.'

'Well . . .' said my father cautiously. Then something inside his head urged, Go on, what've you got to lose? 'Yes,' he said, then repeated it—'Yes!'—jubilant at his own recklessness.

It meant swimming ashore at night to look for spare parts, and hiding below deck during the day, hoping Japanese planes wouldn't spot them. Progress was dangerously slow. They watched as the Union Jack was lowered over Singapore harbour and the Rising Sun raised.

Eventually, their boat limped into Sumatra, where they abandoned it and hitched lifts from Dutch soldiers and Indonesians who were also fleeing the Japanese. They hid in ditches whenever Japanese planes dived low to machine-gun anything that moved. They scrounged food, found abandoned bicycles, and finally made it to a little fishing port in the south of Sumatra. My father told us how he lay on the ground waiting for a boat and watched as mines blew up five out of seven vessels. He caught the sixth boat, and didn't know what happened to the seventh.

—

After my father had recovered, the war claimed him again. He joined the Australian army on a secret mission, teaching Malay to Australian soldiers for an invasion into Japanese-occupied territory that never eventuated.

Nine months after my father's memorable arrival in Armadale, my mother gave birth to their third child, and my second brother, David. She was forty-three; my father was fifty-six. At his army base, somewhere in the north of Australia, he quickly became known as Grandpa.

'Hey, mates, Grandpa's had a baby. No bigger 'n 'is hand. No kiddin'.'

By then we were living back in Perth, near the US Catalina base occupied mainly by black American servicemen. As the streets were full of young women wheeling coffee-coloured babies, I had become convinced that my mother would also produce a coffee-coloured baby.

We went to see my mother in hospital, and I thought she seemed very tired. She waved at us with one hand and then pointed to a crib that was pulled close to her bed. Inside, wrapped in white like a parcel, was a crinkly pink baby who kept making funny noises. He looked as if he was wearing gloves. My mother said that his name was David and he was wearing mittens to stop him scratching his face. His hair was blond, and grew in a few wispy patches—like an old man's, but I didn't tell my mother this. Instead, I offered to wash his nappies—and then wished I hadn't. We had an old-fashioned outdoor copper, heated by firewood, but water was scarce and I wasn't very good at scraping nappy poo into the outdoor dunny before putting the nappies into the copper.

'Yuck,' I'd say, and sometimes retch. But when one of the aunts offered to help, I'd say, 'No', and give the grim smile of a martyr.

AMERICAN SOLDIERS IN AUSTRALIA

After the Japanese bombing of Pearl Harbor, the US Defense Chief, General Dwight D. Eisenhower, decided that the US forces should direct their Pacific campaign from Australia. From December 1941 to August 1945, over a million Americans were stationed in Australia. The American servicemen came with easy manners, money in their pockets, and nylon stockings—'oversexed, overpaid and over here' was how Australians saw them.

One Saturday morning when John, Peta, Judy and I were looking in a pet-shop window, we noticed that two good-looking young American officers were watching us, grinning with goodwill and generosity.

'Hey, kids, whaddya want? Choose. C'mon, choose.'

My brother voted for a tortoise. Peta wanted a Persian kitten. I wanted a puppy. Any puppy. We gazed at the cages, proffered our fingers for licking, sighed with desire.

'Take two,' said a voice that sounded like Frank Sinatra's. And so we went home with two black Pomeranian puppies, both with swollen bellies and fleas. Our mothers made us take them back.

1944

JOHN BECOMES A SOLDIER

Early in 1944, when my brother John was seventeen and still at school, he announced that he was going to enlist in the British army. He had worked out that by the time he arrived in England he would be eighteen, and therefore eligible for military service.

'But not so young—you don't have to go so young,' wailed my mother. And she banged her fists on the table so the dishes and cutlery jumped alarmingly and a knife fell on the floor.

We were having our ritual Sunday morning breakfast, with my mother fussing that she'd overcooked the eggs and my father reading the newspaper. But when John picked up the knife and put his arm around our mother, saying, 'Everyone hates wars; I'll be careful,' my father reacted by pushing his paper angrily across the kitchen table. 'Everyone says they'll be careful—especially the ones that get killed,' he said.

John's cheeks were flushed and I wondered if he was scared. No, I realised, he wasn't scared; he was excited.

He told us he would travel by train to Sydney and from there catch a naval boat to England. We weren't allowed to know what boat, or when it might leave or arrive.

'It's secret,' said John. 'Security and all that stuff.'

'Are you sure you really want to go?' asked my father, reclaiming his newspaper.

'Certain.'

'No heroics?'

'No heroics.'

We waved John goodbye at Perth railway station; the whole Armadale contingent was there, now living in the city. We bought him flowers and chocolate and two detective thrillers, and my mother gave him a black money belt. John wasn't keen to wear it but my father commented that it was the first time in my mother's life that she had shown financial prudence.

My father said, 'Good luck. I'm proud of you!' And the rest of us jumped up and down and sang 'Waltzing Matilda', to my brother's acute embarrassment. He was blinking and wiping his glasses. My mother gripped my elbow and said, 'Don't let me cry.'

Months went by and we didn't hear from John. Then one day we had a letter from the Red Cross saying that he had been in a British army hospital, very ill with pneumonia. The army had failed to issue him with a winter uniform. He took some weeks to recover.

1945

POMS NOT WANTED

Despite the persistent fear of invasion, our lives eventually achieved some kind of normalcy. We were sent to the local primary school in Nedlands, where we looked and talked 'different', as the headmaster kept telling us. All the girls in Grade 6A had 'windswept hair', the latest fashion. But when I tried to look like them by hacking at my fringe, I made matters worse.

The city of Perth was walled in sandbags and draped in flags. Every day we assembled in the school playground to salute our flag and every day we sang the Australian national anthem, 'God Save the King'. We had weekend jobs, we groomed and exercised horses from nearby stables, we learned to surf.

Yet our household was poor and our mothers were often depressed. Doreen was still suffering from tropical sprue. She was very thin and had to eat copious numbers of bananas every day. Yette had heard via a telegram delivered one Friday morning that her husband had died. She had a week of mourning and then insisted life must continue. My mother had just had a baby and was feeling both sick and exhausted. We decided we needed to buy our mothers a present, and with the help of a friendly neighbour we settled on a bottle of gin.

We stole jonquils, freesias and daffodils from municipal gardens, and kangaroo paw from Kings Park. We sold the flowers on street corners or door to door. With the money we bought the gin. Our mothers were worried about where the money came from, but they were delighted to have the end result!

I have another memory of that time. Still of war. Always of war. Closed doors, and the murmurs of my mother comforting women whose husbands had died of starvation and brutality in Japanese prisoner-of-war camps. I hadn't encountered grief like this before. Such swollen eyes and terrible sadness. One day I heard my friend Judy crying. I put my arms around her and stroked her hair, but it didn't bring back her father.

Occasionally, a friend of one of our mothers would come round to our house with a printed letter card she had just received from her husband.

I AM WORKING HEALTHILY. WE HAVE JOYFULLY RECEIVED PRESENT SOME MILK, TEA, MARGARINE AND CIGARETTES FROM THE JAPANESE AUTHORITIES.

This was a standardised Japanese message on all POW letter cards. Two blank lines followed—the sole writing space that prisoners were allowed.

—

When 1945 rolled around we were still in Perth, with no sign of peace or the possibility of going 'home' to Britain. Australia was not very welcoming to British people then. NO POMS WANTED said notices in the windows of Perth's neat suburban houses, with their lines of sprinklers and ordered flowerbeds. When we caught the long green tram that rumbled into the city, and my mother held out her money and asked for Hay Street, conductors would often mimic her accent. 'Hee Street!' they would say, and I would clasp my hands around my knees and pretend I wasn't there.

One reason for the antagonism was that 22,000 young Australian soldiers were prisoners of a war not of their making, locked up in camps that tested them to the limits of their courage and endurance. By the end of the war, one in three had died. Lieutenant-General Gordon Bennett, the Australian commanding officer at the time, had not become a prisoner of war. He escaped with two other officers immediately following the surrender of Singapore and was widely criticised for deserting his men. Whenever my father heard any of these arguments, he would quietly disappear.

By then my father had become a shadow in our lives, a melancholic and brooding man. When he came home from Australian army duties we would hear him in the bathroom, weeping or talking to himself. Sometimes my brother and I would climb a ladder to peer through the window. Often he would be shaving, with lather all over his face, looking incongruously like Father Christmas—a Father Christmas who said over and over again: 'I'm sorry, I'm sorry, I'm sorry.'

Looking back, I think my father was suffering from what is now known as post-traumatic stress disorder. Or perhaps it was survivor guilt. Whatever label you wish to fix on him, he was a deeply unhappy man. Perhaps he questioned the morality of his escape when others had stayed behind and perished, particularly his closest friends. Perhaps he also felt he had betrayed his Asian staff by leaving them to suffer the brutality of the Japanese. Yet how could they have come with him when they had families to protect? Almost certainly he felt guilty, even though he was a civilian and had no obligation to stay. His escape from Singapore would haunt him for the rest of his life. He would talk about his survival having more to do with coincidence or luck than some conscious choice—a chance encounter with a man he had rescued, an instinctive response to say yes, gratitude for his life but an intense sorrow for those who died. When my mother tried talking to him about his despair, he always denied anything was wrong.

8 May 1945

VICTORY IN EUROPE DAY

VE Day, marking the end of the war in Europe, affected my parents profoundly—especially my mother. She was already excitedly talking about 'going home'. My father secretly wanted to stay in Australia; he loved the feeling of freedom he had here, and the fact that nobody knew him so he could be as eccentric as he pleased. But in arguments or discussions that involved Home Sweet Home, I already knew that my mother would win, particularly as the British government would be paying our passages.

Today, when I look at old images of Victory in Europe Day, I remember the radio commentator saying, 'It seemed as if the streets were paved with heads.' More than a million people turned out to celebrate.

'We have never seen a greater day than this,' Churchill proclaimed as he waved one of his famous cigars. 'This is your victory,' said this greatest of leaders, who had urged his people to war but led them back to peace.

But the world was not yet at peace.

On Sunday morning, 6 August 1945, the United States dropped an atomic bomb, code name Little Boy, on Hiroshima, and on 9 August a second bomb, Fat Boy, was dropped on Nagasaki. Emperor Hirohito announced Japan's unconditional surrender to the Allies on 15 August. I cannot recall any family celebration. Both my parents were horrified at the devastation caused by nuclear bombs.

One month later, in September 1945, our family was repatriated to an austere and exhausted Britain. I didn't want to go. By now I had settled in to life in Perth. I had won a scholarship to Perth Modern School, I had made friends, and I was anxious about what might lie ahead if we returned to England. My father also wanted to stay. But my mother insisted we would be less isolated in England, where we still had relatives and friends. As our ship, *Fair Sky*, moved slowly out of the port of Fremantle, a large gathering of passengers stood on the bow of the ship. My father passed me his handkerchief. My mother didn't appear. Did she regret not staying? No, she wanted to be in Europe with a passion that my father never understood. But perhaps she felt mildly guilty at getting her way. I never knew.

6

Repatriated

FINDING HOME

In England we saw the struggles of a country trying to bury its bitterness and start again. Food was still rationed and queues were long.

'What's this?' said my mother. We had stepped off the boat in Plymouth and stumbled into our first Lyons Corner House for a much-needed meal.

'What's this?' she repeated, sticking her fork into a grey crumbly mass thinly smeared on a slice of burnt toast.

'Powdered egg,' I mumbled, remembering boarding school. 'It's disgusting.'

'We're damned lucky to have any kind of eggs,' said my father, sucking on his empty pipe. 'Do shut up, Bea. Either eat it or leave it.'

—

Britain has won the war against Germany, but at immense cost to itself and to the world. A vast human tragedy spreads out across generations and nations. Three years after war has ended, huge areas of cities like London and Birmingham remain bomb sites. Shattered buildings lie scattered like broken teeth. Grimy carriages in the underground, grim unsmiling faces in the streets.

'To walk through the ruined cities of Germany is to feel an actual doubt about the continuity of civilisation,' wrote George Orwell in an essay he called 'Future of a Ruined Germany'.

I reach out my hand to a railing, and realise it is covered in soot. I see people struggling with long queues for food and for jobs. When I walk to post a letter, I pass huddles of homeless people, bunched together against the cold. One old man, coughing, calls out something to me, but I am scared to come too close. His companion is holding a battered sign that says, NO FOOD, NO WORK. And I am ashamed because of my fear.

My father is still without work because no one wants to employ a sixty-one-year-old English rubber planter in the middle of an English winter. He has sunk into Stygian gloom, and barely talks to my mother or to me. I can see him ambling down the dingy passageway of one lodging house after another, his hands in mittens, a blackened pipe sticking out of the top pocket of his tweed jacket, reciting with precision:

I wish I loved the human race;
I wish I loved its silly face;
I wish I liked the way it walks;
I wish I liked the way it talks;
And when I'm introduced to one,
I wish I thought 'What jolly fun!'

51

Whenever he says this, I feel sad. His whole being, the set of his shoulders, his bravura, expresses his disappointment with a life that has left him like an old beached whale unable to find its way back to the open sea.

He has become ever more isolated and will no longer talk about his escape. Gradually, I come to believe that perhaps he has exaggerated the story or even made it up. Our relationship is now reduced to grunts. Once, when I was fifteen, I flew at him with a pair of scissors. He did not punish me but took them from me and continued reading as if I did not exist.

'D'you want to go to the cinema?' he'd say, so my mother and I would grab our coats in excitement and wait by the front door until he appeared, coatless and smoking his pipe. 'I didn't say I wanted to go. I just asked if you wanted to go.'

Yet we were lucky. We had survived two major wars, one in Europe and the other in the Pacific. We had been bombed; chased by German submarines; invaded by the Japanese; my mother escaping; my brother and I evacuated to safety in Perth; my father missing, believed dead, then also escaping. None of us had died, none were wounded, none imprisoned or tortured. Instead, we were part of an ever-swelling diaspora of loss that filled the whole of Europe, spilling out over borders, advancing, pausing, retreating, as millions of people searched for shelter and the hope of starting again.

For us, life in those early years back in England was of endless moves: London, Brighton, Sheffield, Manchester and out into the boondocks of Derbyshire's coal-mining country, looking for work and a home as we wheezed and coughed our way through English winters, clutching at ration cards and joining long and grumpy queues for food.

—

In 1946, we moved from London to Sheffield, where a distant relative, a rotund Yorkshireman who was on the board of John Brown Tractors, suggested that my father might try selling tractors up north, commission on sale. As my father knew nothing about tractors we quickly sank into greater penury, even though we'd optimistically rented a house called Idle Hour, in the village of Hope on the Derbyshire moors. John managed to get leave from the army to help us move.

After weeks of trying to sell tractors, my father decided motorcars might be easier. 'At least I can drive a car,' he said with forced joviality, just before spending his very small amount of Japanese war reparations money on four dubious-looking second-hand cars.

That first winter in England was bitterly cold. Snow piled up in front of our house. Snow covered the four cars. It edged up over their mudguards and clung to their bonnets so that they loomed at us like prehistoric white monsters every time we opened the front door.

The following year we could no longer afford our house in Hope. My father decided to go north to Manchester, hoping to find work there. My mother and I and three-year-old David stayed behind. We tried a couple of boarding houses until my mother found a spartan unfurnished house in Yorkshire. This was grim, scar-faced country dominated by open-cast coal mining. My mother furnished the house with beds from the

Salvation Army and bits and pieces she bought at auctions—including ten commode chairs. I gawked at them, aghast, when I realised what they were.

My mother ignored me. She was busy rolling up the sleeves of one of my father's checked winter shirts—one he had left behind and she was now wearing. 'Commercial travellers are supposed to tell rude jokes and wear white collars and ties,' he had said wryly when he packed his bag and walked off to catch the train that would take him to Manchester. We had waved him goodbye from our front door, a tall, gaunt man, hands in the pockets of a baggy tweed coat, stumbling a little, but still trying to maintain his dignity.

Back in the house, my mother was about to tackle the ten commode chairs. 'Pay attention: this is what we'll do. First, we sterilise the chamber pots with boiling water and disinfectant. When they're clean and dry, we put them back in the chairs, slap on their lids, add a cushion, and there, ladies and gentlemen, we have ten dining room chairs. Going, going, gone! All for ten pounds!'

Next my mother bought a second-hand treadle sewing machine that she used to make curtains and loose covers for sofas and chairs. She had never done this kind of work before, but she said she merely used her common sense. In summer, I helped her pick fruit that we made into jam and sold by the side of the road. She also began to put together a portfolio of drawings and textile designs.

'I might need them,' she said mysteriously.

One Saturday lunchtime, after my mother had been trying to slash back undergrowth in our garden, she said her back was aching and decided to have a bath. So there she was, sitting in a rusty enamel bath in about three inches of lukewarm water, when our drunken Czechoslovakian landlord, Mr Pavlic, entered the house and smashed his way into the bathroom, waving a riding crop. His black boots were muddy; he wore tight beige riding breeches and a black jacket, and smelled of cheap alcohol.

'Madam, where is the fucking rent, madam?' Mr Pavlic shouted with such anger that he lost his balance and nearly fell into the bath.

He righted himself just as my mother rose, naked and majestic, and pointed at the door. 'Leave my house! At once, sir!'

As it was his house, and the rent was overdue, I expected him to hit my mother with his whip. Instead, he lurched his way out of the bathroom and, once safely outside, clicked his heels and bowed. 'Fuck you, madam,' he said and belched. He turned and staggered up the garden path. When he came to the iron gate, he tried to kick it open. It fell off its hinges.

I passed my mother a towel. 'Everything is falling off its hinges,' I said sadly.

Two days after the landlord drama, my mother decided she'd had enough. 'If you're in a sodding mess, you don't have to lie in it as well,' she said. She sold her sewing machine, and with the money bought an imitation Christian Dior suit. It was lovat green with a dark green velvet collar, a nipped-in waist and a long flared skirt. She left a kindly neighbour in charge of me and David, packed a bag, put her portfolio of designs under her arm, and caught a train to London. Within a week she had found a job as a design consultant at a leading textile firm.

'Is the job well paid?' I asked.

'Enough. It's enough.'

My mother persuaded Sheffield High School to let me finish my last two years without paying any fees. I boarded with a school friend whose mother took in washing by wheeling an old battered pram through the streets, calling out: 'Washing, washing, has anybody any washing?' David went to social-worker cousins of my father's in Lancashire and stayed with them for nearly two years. John was promoted to lieutenant and was able to come for visits on periodic leave. And my mother worked, trying to save money to bring us all together again.

My father stayed in Manchester as a commercial traveller selling Christmas cards, but he didn't fit well with what he called 'commercial traveller jokes'. He remained depressed. Occasionally, he would catch the train to Sheffield and take me out to Sunday lunch. All I can remember is the intolerable clinking of cutlery against white plates as we pushed around powdered eggs and sausages, or sausages and powdered eggs, while we searched for words. Any words. We rarely found them.

In 1973, two years after my father died, I found a letter he had written to my mother while I was still at school, and just after we had spent a painful day together.

I have just seen Anne. Everyone tells me she is intelligent, some even say she is attractive. Frankly, I find no glimmer of intelligence, nor would I say she is good-looking. Perhaps, in God's good time she will change—and you know I have little time for God.

I am trying to remember how I felt after I had read the letter. I think I folded it carefully and returned it to my mother's dressing-table drawer. Angry? Yes. Hurt? Yes. But the cuts were not very deep. Both his family and his friends were so used to his periods of depression and sarcasm that mostly we didn't take his remarks too seriously. Perhaps that was the unkindest cut of all.

—

When we first arrived back in England, in October 1945, my father's eldest brother, George, had found us rooms in a boarding house in Hove, East Sussex, near a large Regency hotel he owned, called Sillwood Hall Hotel. George had made his money in Monte Carlo before the war, playing cards. He wore a monocle that kept falling in his lap, and had a nervous tic that had him repeating, 'What-what-what? What?' at the end of most sentences.

His wife, Clarice, played the gee-gees. For days on end, streams of punters would traipse in and out of her bedroom where she would sit up in bed, holding court, her teacup sometimes perilously lodged on her ample bosom. On winning days, she wore a large black hat festooned with roses.

Sunday mornings were reserved for me, her niece; she would read me salacious bits from the *News of the World* and give me pocket money to bet on the horses. My mother found out when she saw me wearing a fancy watch.

'I bought it with my own money,' I said indignantly. 'I bet on a horse called Red, and it won.'

'Well done,' said my father, and hastily left the room. He always kept well away from any hint of family conflict, not realising how much he himself caused. His wish was to go back to his beloved Malaya, or to find an English country garden with roses and a compost heap, with a church nearby where he could sing hymns without necessarily having to believe in God.

London, 1947

WHEEZY'S HOUSE

It was nearly two years before we were all together again. An ancient aunt died and fortuitously left her house to my father. This aunt—my father's oldest sister—was known by my older brother and me as Wheezy because of the strange huffing noises she made whenever she bore down on us, her lips puckered for a kiss. Just before Wheezy died, from something mysteriously called Bright's disease, she remade her will and left her house to my father. She said this was because he neither gambled on the stock exchange nor played the cards like their brother George.

My father and my brother David arrived home at about the same time. I think I was helping to put up curtains while David, then aged four, was chattering away to my father, who was up a ladder and not very happy about it. David stood beneath him, his feet wide apart, his arms crossed. He looked up and said in a determined voice, 'Eeh, father, God'll laff if thee falls dahn and breaks thy bones.'

My father laughed, not God. He laughed so heartily at the broad Lancashire brogue his small son had acquired that he nearly did fall down and break his bones.

At the back of Wheezy's large, ugly, two-storey house, my father had his own generous garden, which he planted with flowers, vegetables and fruit—roses, delphiniums, geraniums, tomatoes, strawberries, everything according to season—and a courtyard where sweet-scented clematis bloomed. It was in a suburb of London called Willesden Green, but my mother got away with calling it Hampstead Heath.

I didn't like Wheezy's house. It was Edwardian, solidly built of dark liver-coloured brick and filled with large pieces of heavily polished mahogany furniture that glowed in the dark. The lights were shaded in burgundy chiffon, fringed with beads. The floors creaked. I found it ugly and forbidding—but at least we now had a home and I felt vaguely guilty when I realised how lucky we were to have anywhere to live.

I had dropped out of two universities because I didn't know what I wanted to do and, anyway, my County of Middlesex grant didn't nearly cover my educational costs. At first, inspired by the intriguing introduction I'd had to adult life courtesy of my aunt Clarice and the *News of the World*, I decided that when I grew up I would become a crime reporter. I was firmly told that if I did that, nice men wouldn't like me. I decided I would be a psychiatrist, and was advised that it would be easier if I became a nurse. So I went to work at one of the large London hospitals where I was officially designated 'a typiste', working in the birth control clinic three days a week and the fertility clinic two days.

Birth control in those days was only for married couples, and was generally limited to brown rubber caps or diaphragms for the 'ladies', and condoms for the 'gentlemen'—which I wasn't supposed to know about, let alone touch. After two weeks I was dismissed, finding that there was a bit more to being an accurate 'typiste' than I had thought. I went home and, feeling fragile, took to my bed, where I stayed for the next three months except for occasional forays to the world outside in search of Cadbury's chocolate bars and 'bath buns' covered in white crystalline sugar.

One night, I wrote to my brother John, who was in the army somewhere in Somalia. I told him I felt I was swimming a long way out from shore in strange and sullen seas. Going nowhere.

'Keep swimming!' he replied, as I knew he would.

My mother had better ideas. 'Why don't you go and work for a man with an interesting job?' she suggested.

I fell out of bed. '*I* want the interesting job.'

I returned to study at a London polytechnic, and worked in its science laboratories, cleaning endless dirty tanks filled with suppurating dogfish floating in formaldehyde. When the time drew near for exams, I realised that I hadn't been to a single science lecture, preferring the English ones instead.

May 1949

POST-WAR PARIS

I decided to go to Paris. Paris would be escape. Paris was 'abroad'. At that stage of Britain's existence in relation to the rest of the world, anywhere that wasn't in the British Isles was Abroad or The Continent. Paris had an identity of its own. And so I hurried downstairs looking for someone who would listen to my proposal. My mother was sympathetic—probably because I used the word 'adventure' and for the first time in a long while sounded excited. My mother was all for adventure and excitement. She wanted me to be happy. She wanted me to be independent.

'Always be independent, darling,' said she who ended up having Alzheimer's and tragically losing her own independence. But all this was in years to come. Today, I know nothing of it. Today, I am eighteen, nearly nineteen, and I am going to Paris. I will hitchhike with a friend called Denis who is in England on a Beaverbrook Scholarship for young Jamaican journalists.

Denis is worldlier than I am and a little older. We are good friends and my father trusts him, which makes everyone breathe a sigh of relief. Otherwise my father would have been stomping up and down the kitchen, prophesying carnal doom and a coffee-coloured baby.

'No risks,' commands my father, which is his way of saying, 'No sex.'

'No, sir,' says Denis.

My father pats him on the back and says, 'Good man.' He starts to walk away and then turns, awkwardly shifting from one foot to the other. 'Look after her, will you?' he says. 'Good man.'

Both the good man and my good father appear oblivious to my presence.

'I can look after myself, thanks,' I say as I make a noisy exit, slamming the door.

Our first lift is in a baker's van, driven by a middle-aged man and his wife who are clearly intensely curious about us. Denis has long black legs and wears brief white shorts. I am in a floral print dress with a straw hat and look as if I am going to a garden party. We are both very young. We are not lovers, but they clearly think we are. When we leave them—halfway to Dover—the woman pulls me to one side and says, 'Be careful, dear. He may be a good-looker, and a

61

good boy for all I know, but you don't want no half-caste babes. Nothing but trouble.'

At Dover, we catch a cross-Channel ferry that buckles and groans at every wave, and tosses its passengers around like some wild animal trying to offload an obnoxious human burden. No one falls overboard. They heave vomit instead. I am also sick, but I don't care. I know this is the time when everything is to be explored, every sensation, every challenge, every new idea. Denis leaves me in Paris to head south for Rome and I find a room in a small hotel on the Left Bank, in a narrow street called the Passage de la Petite-Boucherie that doesn't have any butcher's shops but does have bakeries, cafes and a corner bistro where I can live off bread, cheese and soup that smells of herbs and spices. I light fires in my metal bidet to keep myself warm, and bluff my way into a job with the French-American magazine *Realities*.

I stand before Gareth Windsor, one of the best-known editors of post-war journalism, and say, 'My name is Anne Deveson and I want a job.' I smile hopefully. I am tall, I have a wasp waist and you could say I am a cross between a milkmaid and an aspiring Juno. 'I can type, I can speak some French, I want to be a journalist and I'd be good.'

The typing issue worries me somewhat, but I had been giving myself speed lessons in London on the antiquated machine my father had picked up in a market on Hampstead Heath.

Gareth Windsor does give me a job—on a three-month project helping a Hungarian economist, Tibor Mende, who has just written a book on Eastern Europe's post-war industrial turmoil. I am to type, check his English, and help with editing. I work by day, and occasionally raid his fridge for food. At night

I stand in crowded jazz clubs smoking Gauloises and listening to Charlie Parker, Coleman Hawkins, Juliette Gréco, and countless young French jazz musicians. I have exchanged my floral print dresses for black stovepipes and black jumpers. I have dyed my hair blonde, cropped it short and brushed it forward in Napoleonic style. I am still not any good at cutting hair.

'Dance with me,' commands a man in the smoky nightclub. He has dark curly hair, dark eyes, and an intensity that both alarms and excites.

'Where are you from?' I say in my most sophisticated voice.

'Israel. You?'

'England.'

'I have killed many English.'

'Oh really?' We continue dancing. This is the kind of post-war dancing that's face to face, chest to chest, lead with the legs and not much space in between.

'I want to know you better,' he murmurs.

I think this means a much-needed meal. He means bed. I decline and then regret it once I am alone in my very small room in this very small hotel. I am living in a city where young people are trying to shake off the horror of war years and find freedom. Freedom to breathe, freedom to speak, freedom to love.

And what is freedom? And is this love? I would wonder as I dived into dark corners of dark rooms where bodies mingled and headaches mounted as wine bottles emptied. Somewhere in this bacchanalia were youthful spirits seeking love and only rarely finding it.

One day M. Mende asked me to type a letter to Bertrand Russell, the eminent British philosopher and peace activist, requesting that he write a foreword for Mende's book on Eastern

Europe. So there I was, sitting at a pavement table outside the famous Deux Magots cafe where Jean-Paul Sartre, Simone de Beauvoir and Albert Camus gathered with their followers and friends, avidly reading Russell's first anti-nuclear writing. It was titled 'The Bomb and Civilisation' and he had written it in 1945, just after America had dropped the atomic bomb on Hiroshima. Russell's paper curled in the breeze and ash from my cigarette blew across the table as I read:

> The prospect for the human race is sombre beyond all precedent. Mankind are faced with a clear-cut alternative: either we shall all perish, or we shall have to acquire some slight degree of common sense. A great deal of new political thinking will be necessary if utter disaster is to be averted . . . As I write, I learn that a second bomb has been dropped on Nagasaki.

The enormity of those wartime events struck me deeply as I sat at the Deux Magots pouring endless spoonfuls of sugar into my coffee, remembering what I would rather forget. How, in an instant, one small bomb had exterminated every vestige of life throughout four square miles of a crowded city.

I wanted to know more about this man, Bertrand Russell, who made such strong and terrible pronouncements. Who would listen to him, take heed? My questions may have been naïve, but they came from a growing realisation that here was a man who dared to challenge the insanity of war, and that individual citizens can take up great moral and political issues. I was already being influenced by the writings of Sartre and de Beauvoir and their existentialist proposition that individuals are free to make choices—or not to make them. De Beauvoir's book *Le Deuxième Sexe* had just been published, in June 1949, and I was struggling to read it in French.

Once Tibor Mende's book was completed, and Bertrand Russell's foreword had been delivered, my work was finished. I'd hardly call myself a rebel without a cause. In fact, it made me aware that I was a young woman without a cause. I didn't feel I belonged anywhere. But where did I want to belong? I sat on the footpath in St-Germain-des-Prés—which was then the kind of place where people could sit on footpaths—leaned against the trunk of a beautiful chestnut tree, listening to the music of a language that I only partially understood.

Paris had escaped the worst of the bombing because it had capitulated to Germany, but people were still suffering. As in other cities that had been occupied, resistance and bravery challenged collaboration and shame. Families were torn apart as collaborators were hunted down and punished by death or public humiliation.

One morning I witnessed an *épuration sauvage*—punishment for collaboration with the enemy. I was walking along the Left Bank—just up from the River Seine—and was about to turn in to my street when I saw ahead of me a crowd watching as a young woman was tied to a chair. She was struggling, spitting at the man who bound her, shouting, '*Vous n'avez pas raison!*' *You are wrong.* She winced as he slapped her face—thwack, thwack. Another man, a stocky character with bulging eyes, pulled a cutthroat razor out of the pocket of his black jacket and began tugging at the young woman's hair, jerking it so her throat and head were pulled back as he swept the razor across her head. Clouds of silky black hair began falling to the ground.

The crowd cheered and shouted abuse as if they were watching a public hanging, or the beheading of Marie Antoinette, whose own hair had probably tumbled to the ground.

I wondered what this young woman had done. Given away secrets? Slept with a German soldier? Or two, or three? Handed over a Jew? Or several? Betrayed a French resistance cell?

I would never know. I watched in horrified fascination as her hair fell and her head was laid bare. Such a naked head, blue and bleeding, and her teeth chattering as she tried to push her way through the jeering crowds. Next thing, someone was setting fire to the mass of rich dark hair that lay coiled on the pavement. It smouldered, like a black snake burning, pain rising.

I ran to the post office, my own teeth chattering as I fumbled in my bag for a pen and scrawled a telegram to my mother.

LEAVING PARIS ARRIVING SOON ANNE

Then I sat in a pavement cafe, sickened by the brutality I had just observed, yet also recognising the brutality of betrayal. I ordered a pernod and realised I had been captivated by the beauty of Paris. I had looked, listened, read, asked questions, yet never fully recognising the significance of being a stranger in another land—of belonging, yet not quite belonging, perhaps never belonging.

—

I felt the same some months later when I was in our kitchen in London and came across pictures of survivors from Nazi concentration camps picking fleas out of each other's hair. They were so emaciated, they looked as if all flesh had vanished and only bones remained.

I flapped my hands helplessly. 'How could we do this?' I shouted aloud. 'How could we treat each other in such cruel and terrible ways?' But we could. And we had.

Yet I also began to understand what good can be done, if the will is there. The year before I went to Paris, 1948, had been Europe's coldest winter since 1880. Thousands had died. Countries were destitute and desperate. Several ideas to aid the rebuilding of Europe had been proposed, from inflicting harsh reparations on Germany to the US giving aid.

In January in that coldest of years, US President Harry Truman appointed George Marshall Secretary of State; in just a few months, Marshall and others had crafted the Marshall Plan—or the European Recovery Program (ERP)—which set about rebuilding the economies and spirit of Western Europe. Marshall was convinced that national economies had to be revitalised. Sixteen nations, including Germany, became part of the program. The same aid was offered to the USSR and its allies, but they did not accept it. During the years of the ERP, member nations experienced economic growth of between 15 and 25 per cent. Agricultural production sometimes exceeded pre-war levels.

Marshall's approach was in stark contrast to the punitive aims of the Treaty of Versailles following the First World War, under which both Japan and Germany were made to suffer for their declaration and prosecution of war. Winston Churchill described the Marshall Plan as 'the most unselfish act by any great power in history'.

A Parisian who rented out deck chairs on the Champs-Elysées told a friend, 'Without Marshall aid probably very few people would be sitting down. Most of them would be rioting and bashing each other over the head with my chairs.'

Now, as I sit in my home in Sydney, Australia, typing this some sixty years later, while the dog snores in gentle rhythm with my tapping on the keyboard, I reflect that generosity and justice remain essential elements in peace-making.

'Real power is about generosity. Real power is about being bigger than revenge,' wrote American playwright Eve Ensler in a book called *Stop the Next War Now*. 'It requires every part of our being to say, "I'm not going to hit you back. I'm going to take a breath and find what within me is larger and has the power to enlighten . . . this possibility of violence as a solution to anything is not tolerable, permissible, or sane."'

On the eve of the 1945 San Francisco Conference to draft a charter for the newly formed United Nations, Mahatma Gandhi, the great champion of non-violent protest, delivered a memorably strong message about peace:

> There will be no peace for the Allies or the world unless they shed this belief in the efficacy of war and its accom-panying terrible deception and fraud, and are determined to hammer out a real peace based on the freedom and equality of all races and nations.
>
> Peace must be just. In order to be that, it must be neither punitive nor vindictive. Germany and Japan should not be humiliated. The strong are never vindictive. Therefore the fruits of peace must be shared equally. The effort will then be to turn them into friends. The allies can prove their democracy by no other means.

7

Work, Love, Family

England, 1950

LOOKING FOR WORK

A month after I returned to London from Paris, I was sitting in our kitchen, planning to write to local newspapers to seek work. Christmas was over, and a few coloured streamers remained tacked to the mantelpiece, tumbling over a bowl of chestnuts that we still hadn't roasted.

My father was hanging around, restlessly walking up and down. 'If you don't hurry up you'll be sitting at that table ten years from now,' he said in his gloomiest voice.

I ignored him, and gazed at the bare branches of a young oak tree tapping against our window. I needed to find work so I began my letter writing. And I was lucky: the *Kensington News* in the Royal Borough of Kensington was seeking a junior reporter. The paper boasted England's only female editor, a confident bright-eyed woman called Barbara Denny. At my interview, we talked together for almost an hour, then she gave me the job. Running home I nearly fell over with excitement.

I started work two weeks later. On my first day, I found myself in a small Dickensian building near Notting Hill Gate. Finance and marketing were on the bottom floor, editorial on the top. Printing took place in a cottage separated from us by a laneway called Rabbit Row.

The print was set by hand, letter by letter, in wooden formes that were the same size as the finished pages. When all the pages had been completed, the formes would be locked down, placed in barrows, and wheeled around to us for proofreading.

I had been there for two weeks when I was given my first front-page story, a safe and easy account of the latest Civil Defence campaign—colloquially known as 'CD'—to be opened by King George in Kensington Town Hall.

I wrote the story. I wrote the headlines. The editor passed them both. Copy was sent to the printers and returned by wheelbarrow. The paper was printed and my story was the lead.

'Better get upstairs quick. She's furious,' said Gus, the messenger boy, as I arrived for work early the following day.

'Why?'

'Never seen her so mad.' He grinned.

Upstairs, Barbara Denny was drumming her fingers on the desktop. 'Read!' she commanded, pushing a copy of the paper towards me.

'I have. I thought it was fine,' I said modestly.

'Read!' she repeated. 'Aloud.'

'"King Supports VD",' I read. I gasped. 'But I wrote, "King Supports CD!"'

'And who was the last person who read the pages?'

'I was.'

'And therefore whose responsibility is this?'

'Mine,' I said in a wretched voice.

'Buckingham Palace has already demanded an explanation. You are to draft a letter and hand it to me within an hour.'

Suddenly, I felt absurdly vulnerable, as if all the guns of Buckingham Palace were aimed at me—as if the King himself might appear, waving a black umbrella, shouting, 'OFF WITH HER HEAD!'

At the end of the day I crept towards the door, hoping no one would notice me leave.

'Good work,' shouted a cheerful voice. The accountant was waving a copy of the paper. 'Sell out! Best takings we've ever had. Well done!'

—

As the *Kensington News* had only two editorial staff, I covered everything and anything, from street markets to West End theatre, films and art galleries, local council meetings and crime. One day I might interview actor Laurence Olivier; the next, artist Lucian Freud. Two weeks after the VD disaster, I was sent to report on London's famous Acid Bath murders, which fascinated and horrified me, but I asked so many questions that I became fearful that one of the older cops—who had asked where I lived—could be the murderer in disguise, waiting to strangle me.

1952

FOOTLOOSE IN EUROPE

I worked at the *Kensington News* for almost two years and then left to see more of Europe. At the time it seemed as if all the young people of Europe were on the move, as if war were forgotten and the future was ours. Hitchhiking was still considered safe, as long as you used common sense. In the south of France, I was given a lift by two young newlywed Americans, who were aghast to hear I was travelling on my own. They weren't aware of the reckless need for freedom that the war had inspired in European youth. The Americans invited me to be their guest for several days.

'It's Noël Coward's house. We thought it would be kind of cute to rent it. See what it's like.'

It was beautiful. It looked out across the Mediterranean; its rooms were vast, its gardens exquisite. I stayed a week, and then made my way along the coast to Italy and then to Spain.

These were heady times: they included going to Italy to cover the Venice Film Festival, falling in love with a young Greek lawyer who was about to study in Cambridge, and beginning a seven-year on-again, off-again affair with him that ended painfully for both of us.

I returned to London and signed up with an exclusive West End secretarial agency. My first assignment was to work for Winston Churchill's son, Randolph Churchill. He was both drunk and rude. I stayed for one day and never returned. Next, I was assigned to food writer Elizabeth David, by then a large woman who kept all her recipes in a trunk under her bed and had me spending much of my time on all fours retrieving them. Sometimes she let me help eat the results—after which she would write her column.

London, 1954

BARBARA IS DIFFERENT

I realised I was fretting to get back into newspapers. I mentioned this to the elegant head of the West End agency, who sent me to a woman called Barbara Wace, the first woman to report on the Allied invasion of Europe in the Second World War.

'Barbara is different,' the posh woman said. 'She is my friend and I think you two will get on. You will be lucky to work with her.'

I *was* lucky to work with her. I went for lunch, stayed for supper, and ended up working with Barbara in a partnership that lasted seven years, until I moved to Australia. She lived just off Fleet Street, in a small flat above the Clachan pub at Old Mitre Court, where she would sometimes receive mail addressed to 'Almighty Court'. She had moved there because it was close to her work and could be reached quickly during the Blitz, in 1940 and 1941, when London was bombed by the German Luftwaffe. For fifty-seven consecutive nights the city was bombarded. More than a million houses were destroyed or damaged and more than 20,000 civilians were killed, but the Blitz did not achieve its intended goal of demoralising Britain into surrender.

Barbara's flat was a haven for anyone who could manage the ninety-six stairs to the front door. The key was usually stuffed in a sock and thrown out of her window. On my first visit, I leaned panting against her front door and rang what looked like a cowbell.

'I'm cooking kedgeree,' called out a cheerful voice. Kedgeree was a traditional British breakfast from colonial India, and consisted of boiled eggs, smoked haddock, bay leaves, basmati rice, and anything else you might want to add. Barbara would serve it for breakfast, lunch or dinner, and because she added so many other spicy ingredients she laughingly called it 'muckmuck'.

She had travelled widely as a girl, living in Germany, France and England, and staying with her father when he was vice-president of the Saar Boundary Commission, responsible for deciding on the Franco–German border after the First World War.

That first day we met, I looked around at treasures from all over the world: Afghan rugs, Indian cushions, a Moroccan bedspread, Mexican pottery, French and Italian paintings and prints, books, journals and more books. She said she needed help with unanswered letters, unfinished assignments, unfinished filing and unread notes. Her flat was often in a mess, but it didn't interfere with her effervescent spirit, her kindness and her generosity.

Barbara had a magic capacity for making friends—eminent explorers and stranded MPs often shared floor space with homeless teenagers, and her small flat was a mecca for genera-tions of children, though she never had any of her own. 'I left it too late,' she said ruefully, but she would think nothing of taking ten children to the circus or the theatre and then bringing them back for dinner.

Barbara's life had been rich in experience, although she was often so diffident and modest that she would brush off the most extraordinary of happenings as if they were a non-event.

In July 1944, when she was thirty-six, Barbara became the first woman journalist assigned to cover the Allied invasion of France. Before she left, she was given special protective underwear, and received a cable from her bureau chief: KEEP OUT OF DANGER SPOTS THIS IS AN ORDER.

One month later, she covered the liberation of Paris for *Life* magazine, and immediately after that the ferocious forty-six-day siege of Brest in Brittany. Apart from the fighting and danger of snipers, there were other problems. The only available toilet was a forty-seater—okay for soldiers, not so good for one solo female. One night, when she was sleeping in a barn, her clothes were stolen. Her subsequent dispatch caused much merriment in the offices of Associated Press: LOST SKIRT BREST FALLEN. The telegram went around the world.

After the war, Barbara's knowledge of German helped her get a job with the British Embassy in Berlin. During the 1936 Olympic Games, she sat only a few feet from Hitler when Jesse Owens, the black American sprinter, won the hundred-yard dash. She said she would never forget the disgust on Hitler's face at that particular moment, or the mesmeric effect of the crowd at Nazi rallies chanting '*Heil* Hitler!'. She told me, 'At moments, I'd feel close to being drawn in, on the verge of leaping up and joining the frantic saluting. It was horrible.'

It was through Barbara that I came to know, and work for, almost everyone in the newspaper world—from the *New York Times* and the *New York Herald Tribune* to the *Atlantic Monthly*, the *National Geographic* and the *Guardian* (then known as the *Manchester Guardian*).

One morning I saw an advertisement in the London *Times* for people interested in joining a small group going to Albania.

Barbara and I replied. The advertisement had been placed by John, a rich young dairy farmer from the north of England who had long nurtured a love affair with Albania. Since Mussolini's invasion in 1939, Albania had been closed to ordinary travellers from the 'free world'. When the Second World War ended, the Iron Curtain clamped down even more tightly and access only became possible in 1957, when we, a pioneer group of up to twelve people, were unexpectedly allowed to visit as tourists.

We were a strange party: a retired naval officer; a handsome young peer of the realm; a grumpy old man we named Herr Schmidt (definitely a spy), who sucked lemon drops all day and was the only one who travelled first class; a couple of glamorous women who could have come straight out of a spy thriller; an Australian film-maker who thumped after everyone like a bad-tempered rhinoceros; and Barbara and me. Rumours spun around the group: we were spies; John was a spy; the Russians were going to arrest and shoot us; the Russians would only shoot Barbara and me.

Our organiser—John of the soft white hands and consider-able wealth—was probably the most suspected, although I think his motives for arranging the trip were romantic ones. He had fallen in love with Albanian music and Albanian history—particularly the story of the tall and handsome King Zog, who survived fifty-seven assassination attempts before his mother assumed supervision of the royal kitchen. Zog was King of Albania from 1928 to 1939. He, his wife Geraldine and their two-day-old son were forced to flee when Mussolini's troops invaded the country in 1939. 'Oh God, my time as king was so short. Too short,' John told me Zog had said.

Our train took us to Venice then Trieste, where we caught a boat that sailed down the Adriatic coast. We left the boat at Ulcinj, which was still under Tito's control, and wandered around the harbour. An open-air cafe had bare-topped wooden tables and waiters in crumpled white jackets. Men in cloth caps sat silently drinking brightly coloured liqueurs. Somewhere a gramophone played 'Parlez-moi d'amour'. Strings of fairy lights and giant pink hollyhocks made the scene somehow improbable. In the streets outside, women sat in Turkish pantaloons and yashmaks, veils thrown back. An old man in a pink fez squatted in the sun, horse-drawn buses with creaking wheels sent up clouds of dust, and sleek Russian cars with lace curtains at the windows moved smoothly down the wide main boulevard. As the cars approached us, the black-booted policeman on point duty would flash his immaculate white-gloved hands as if he were conducting an opera.

Relations between Yugoslavia and Albania had long been tense, and so when we came to the bridge that would take us from Yugoslavia into Albania we were searched, and then ordered to walk in single file, eyes straight ahead. 'No talk,' said the Yugoslav soldier who cradled a machine gun. The soldiers in Albania also cradled guns. As I walked, I wondered why the hell I'd come. Suppose this was a trap? Suppose we were harbouring a real spy? Suppose one of the soldiers opened fire? But nothing dramatic happened; for a second, this seemed almost a let-down.

8

Orstralia

RETURN TO AUSTRALIA

One Friday night I was with a group of journalist friends on a rooftop in Fleet Street, having a drink and catching up on our news. A few of them had heard I was thinking of leaving England. They began asking me questions—until Denise butted in. Denise was the editor of a London magazine for which I wrote, and she threw a question at me with her yeasty North Country accent. 'Anne, Annie my love, are you sure you're not daft going to Australia?'

Everyone turned to hear my answer, but I didn't give one. I was realising how much I would miss London if I went ahead with my plans to marry a well-known Australian broadcaster called Ellis Blain, and live in Tasmania.

'Are there any theatres in Orstralia, do you suppose?' This question came from a journalist who wrote for one of the social pages. 'You'll have to get married, of course. And if you have a baby you might be wise to come home.'

'I'm not pregnant,' I snapped.

'Mind you don't pick up any of those terrible Orstralian accents,' she said.

'Thanks. I've been vaccinated.'

I felt ill at ease. One night a few days after I had told my parents I was thinking of living with Ellis and leaving for Australia, my father had started his usual restless pacing up and down the hallway of our house. 'How d'you think people will accept the fact you're not yet married? Hobart isn't London, you know.' He tapped his fingers on his pipe. 'And how d'you know this chap isn't a bounder?'

I sighed, as my normally robust mother said, 'Oh dear, oh dear,' and dabbed her eyes.

—

I had been introduced to Ellis by Elise Blumann, an elderly artist from Western Australia, a former neighbour of ours who had travelled on the same cargo ship as Ellis and decided we would enjoy each other's company.

'You will share the same interests,' she said with determination.

We did share many of the same interests, but his intensity alarmed me. When he took me out to dinner for the first time, he kept saying, 'Anne Devastation, Anne Devastation, you will change my life.'

As I didn't want to change his life or anyone else's, I avoided him for a while by saying I was working.

'I like him but he gives me a headache,' I told a friend.

Eventually I agreed to meet him on Sunday morning for a walk across Hampstead Heath. Ellis was sixteen years older than me and was an intelligent and interesting man. We talked about his love of music and literature. He listened to an abbreviated account of my Grecian love affair. We discussed life on a cargo ship, what it was like being a refugee, and the time his parents sent him to Bedales, a boarding school in England, where he was told by a head prefect: 'In England we always wear our outdoor shoes outdoors, and our indoor shoes indoors.' His mother was taking singing lessons in Europe—apparently she had a beautiful voice.

Ellis was an Australian with an impeccable English accent, and this was a time in Australia when nearly all senior jobs were given to Australians with impeccable English accents or, better still, to English. But Ellis wasn't intimidated by the English. When he invited me to drive around England with him, exploring the countryside in spring, I was tempted, but when my headache flashed a warning, I declined.

After Ellis left on his trip, he sent me daily postcards. Finally he returned to London with a bottle of Dom Perignon, an armful of red roses, and a toolkit with which to mend my broken bedside light. The Dom Perignon won the day.

Ellis wanted to marry me. I said no, he was already married— he should go home and work things out. Looking back, none of this was sensible. But we are seldom sensible when we are in love. Sensible would have been to know each other better. Sensible would have been to ensure his wife's feelings. Sensible would have been to introduce Ellis to my parents and my friends. Sensible would have been better for both our sakes, his as much as mine.

—

We began our life together in Hobart, where Ellis was the newly appointed program director for the ABC in Tasmania. I met Ellis's children, who were friendly and helpful. And I discovered, at first to my amusement, and then to my dismay, that Ellis was obsessive compulsive and would not let me make the bed, nor sit on the bed, nor object if he wanted to sweep the floor at least three times a day. Cushions on sofas had to be placed in straight lines. Occasionally he tried to do the same with people.

No matter. In the early days, I was delighted to have Ellis make the bed and clean the house. In return I did the cooking and learned how to make yoghurt. I was happy. I felt loved and I enjoyed giving love. But from the beginning, there was a hiccup. Ellis's cousin was the lord mayor of Hobart, and while he and his wife were warm and welcoming, at the end of our first meal at their house he said, 'Anne, we'd love to ask you to meet some of our friends, but I'm afraid we can't until you're married.'

The embargo grew, and as I became increasingly isolated I remembered my father's warning.

One cold day, I went to see the Tasmanian manager of the ABC, who greeted me wringing his hands. 'I'm so sorry, Miss Deveson,' said this oleaginous man, 'I can't invite you inside. But when you are married, it will be my very great pleasure.' He gave an embarrassed cough.

I stared at him. 'That's ridiculous,' I said lamely. As I walked away, I wondered if I would have been similarly treated if I were a man.

The following week, an unknown person threw red paint on our front door.

Life in Tasmania was difficult. It taught me that if you stray outside the boundaries of society by flouting convention, there is usually a price to pay. And that my father had probably been right. We moved to Sydney.

—

Sydney was different, Sydney was sun, new friends and, later, building a house overlooking the calm of Pittwater at Clareville Beach. A family of koalas lived in a eucalyptus tree just outside our kitchen door.

In the ABC newsroom in Sydney, the news editor—a gruff, stocky man—looked at me with some amazement when I said I didn't want to work for the *Women's Hour* program. I wanted to cover news and current affairs, as I had done in London.

'Well,' he said slowly, grinding out every word, 'I've never used a woman before. I'll have to use you first and see how it feels.'

He used me and was pleased but then sent me to the women's program because he felt women belonged in women's programs. Someone had unkindly dug up an ancient ABC regulation that said, 'Wives of Serving Officers could only have three engagements a year.' As the de-facto wife of a Serving Officer, I felt as though I was in a scene from *The Mikado*. But it wasn't where I wanted to be.

There was plenty to talk about and plenty to show. Behind our neat picket fences of the sixties and seventies, a multitude of human rights abuses were occurring. Wife-bashing was a musical-hall joke. Child abuse was largely ignored because children were seen as the property of their parents—the rest of us could mind our own business. Rape rarely came to court because it wasn't seen as a crime: it was the woman's fault. Child sexual assault was well and truly tucked away and denied. Not long ago I came across some old notes for a television script I had begun writing:

> Abortion is a crime, and most commonly is a backyard butcher's job: one hundred pounds in ten-pound notes, put 'em in a brown paper bag and keep your mouth shut, girlie. Abortion is illegal in every state except South Australia, and then women need to have lived there for two consecutive months. The scenario looks like this:
>
> 'Enter a grey grubby building just off a busy Melbourne street, take a deep breath, try to ignore sobs and cries coming from a long line of cubicles, all occupied, then comes your turn, on to a surgical bed, look no gloves, out to it, wake to it, leave ASAP, sick for the next two or three days with a high temperature, abortion doctor says possibly septicaemia, come back if it gets worse.'

People with disabilities were dismissed as *loonies*, *spazzos*, *crips* and *fruitcakes*. Poverty was widespread and the only escape for many people was smoking or drinking. When I made a film about poverty in the 1960s, the then Minister for Social Welfare told me in an interview that charity is the right response. I played a line from *Oliver Twist*: 'Please, sir, I want some more.' Tertiary education was only available to the rich or very clever. Capital punishment and corporal punishment were still legal. Racism, sexism and homophobia were rampant. Homosexuals were ridiculed, abused, imprisoned. Words were hurled through the air like stones: *poofters, queers, pansies, dykes, lesos.*

—

Our first child, Jonathan, was born in 1961, and had a cerebral haemorrhage at birth. He cried for at least six months. I remember feeding him during the night and gazing into the darkness of his eyes, trying to give strength to his being and willing him well again.

Three years later, in 1964, Georgia was born in hospital—so speedily that I delivered her myself with no one else in the room.

'Doctor will be very displeased,' said an uppity nurse.

Joshua, our youngest, came in 1968. He was eleven and a half weeks premature and weighed less than a kilogram.

All three children had made dramatic entries into the world, but because we could afford childcare I managed to juggle work and children without too much difficulty and found that I loved being a mother. I felt in awe of their life force and how quickly they grew and learned—even Joshua, the little one who spent the first three months of his life in a humidicrib. When he finally came home from hospital, he roared his displeasure night and day, which made me want to roar back on occasion, but it felt as if we were all taking some strange and unpredictable journey together—on a sailing boat with wet nappies as our sails.

—

From the mid-sixties my working life blossomed. I was one of the first two women to have my own current affairs program on radio. I had a bi-weekly column for the Sydney *Sun*. And over a period of several years, I made numbers of groundbreaking documentaries for Channel 7—about the funeral industry, unmarried mothers, homosexuality, poverty, autism, mental illness, children with disabilities, homelessness. Why the focus on social issues? I think because my radio programs gave me an opportunity to hear the voices of people from all around Australia: people struggling with poverty; women living in fear of violence; women suffering isolation and loneliness; children and adults with scant education; Aboriginal children with even less. Many of these were stories of government neglect and of the harshness of a society that could make young unmarried women surrender their newborn babies without ever seeing them.

The swinging sixties

LOVE NOT WAR

Meantime, the world was rocking—rocking with the sounds of rock'n'roll, rocking as young people around the world challenged the conventional meanings given to life, challenged sound, challenged music. The 1960s became synonymous with new, radical and subversive trends of thinking and behaviour which continued to develop into the 1990s and beyond. In Africa, radical political change began in the 1960s as thirty-two countries gained independence from their European colonial rulers. In the United States, John F. Kennedy pushed for social reforms such as civil rights for African Americans and healthcare for the elderly and the poor. For his idealism and his energy he was assassinated.

But then there were so many acts of political violence: the assassination of Bobby Kennedy, the killing of draft resisters, the slaughter of young white upholders of black civil rights, the assassination of Martin Luther King. Violent memories return, even though I live on the other side of the globe.

If I think back to this period, there are moments when it becomes acutely painful even though the movement itself brought a liberation of thinking and behaviour—sometimes as a stream of new ideas, sometimes a river, sometimes an ocean—reminding us that revolutions can occur without mass killing.

There were many inspiring acts. In 1955, Rosa Parks sat in the 'whites only' section of an Alabama bus, and challenged racial segregation; in 1958, the Campaign for Nuclear Disarmament was founded in the United Kingdom; in 1964, Martin Luther King was awarded the Nobel Peace Prize; and, in 1969, two million people marched across the United States as part of the Vietnam War moratorium.

And then we come to the music: Bob Dylan and his first performance with an electric guitar; Pink Floyd, whom my son Jonathan used to listen to, over and over again until, one day, Pink Floyd changed me as it sang through my mind and body—and that without any other drugs for assistance. Marijuana I found messy—which gives away my age—and I became impatient at the sight of rows of chilled-out people giggling and staring vacantly into space. LSD was more interesting—that extraordinary elasticity with time, that intensity of images and sounds—but I was too scared to take it more than two or three times and never when I was anywhere near home. The Beatles: I enjoyed The Beatles, but not as much as I enjoyed Pink Floyd. And like so many millions of others, I fell in love with Leonard Cohen.

By the second half of the decade, a revolution had begun. Young people were rebelling against the conservative norms of the time. A counterculture was created throughout much of the western world. It began as a reaction against the social conformity of the fifties, and extended into a strong revolt against US involvement in the Vietnam War. From this came movements towards social liberation in its broadest sense: the sexual revolution, the questioning of authority, demands for more freedoms and rights for women and minorities. Feminism gained momentum in the early sixties and spread across the world. Gay rights and gay pride followed not too far behind but took much longer to be acknowledged. By the late 1960s, psychedelic drugs were more widely used as young people turned on, tuned in, and dropped out—sometimes, tragically, with drug overdoses.

The ammunition of this revolution was music, not guns. Around the world, young people were urging 'Make Love Not War' as they challenged conventional ways of thinking and being in the world. 'Make Love Not War' extended far beyond individual love into making love with society, a society that young people hoped fervently to change as they tried to escape the drab social conformity of the fifties.

Yet many older people—like my father—desperately wanted to drop back into an untroubled suburban life after the horrors and deprivations of war. At one level, he could see the need for change; at another, he was tired.

I was visiting my parents in London and we were having breakfast in the courtyard garden when my mother remarked how amazed she was at all the black families that had moved into their neighbourhood. 'Why, they keep their children so clean!' she said brightly as she snipped a dying red rose from one of the rose bushes in the garden at the back of the house.

My father looked at her in alarm. 'What's that song you're all singing?' he asked me. 'Something about the times they are a-changing? Well, they need to change. Tell your mother what's happening in the world. She hasn't caught on.'

So I took my mother to London's Carnaby Street where she clapped her hands with delight. It wasn't what my father had in mind, but as he had seemed to be about to deliver a lecture on all the African countries that had gained their independence in the 1960s, I thought she might need an escape.

In Carnaby Street, shop windows were filled with vibrant colour—purple capes, orange stockings, paisley bell-bottom pants, emerald green and yellow hats . . . clothes that gave people permission to play in a technicolour world. I bought my mother a vividly coloured cape and, for me, brown and black stovepipe pants. In the King's Road in Chelsea, groups of young men paraded in body-hugging shirts with scarves and very tight pants.

—

It was also a painful time for me because this was when my son Jonathan first showed signs of developing schizophrenia. He was fourteen years old and I would spend my afternoons cycling around the neighbourhood, looking for his hide-outs, then looking for the joints he had smoked or was about to smoke, and recognising that while his friends would only get mildly stoned, Jonathan's response came with mounting agitation.

In 1978, when he was seventeen years old, Jonathan was given a diagnosis of paranoid schizophrenia, admitted to hospital, put into striped flannel pyjamas and given so much medication that he walked and talked like a zombie.

When he wasn't psychotic, Jonathan was gentle. He was tall and thin, like a reed swaying in a gale. His hair was long and blond and unkempt. He held his pants up by string and his feet were bare as he padded across Sydney Harbour Bridge—there and back, there and back, talking to himself and to the demons that plagued his broken mind. Whenever I saw him, I would want to weep.

These were the days when we were all supposed to be living in Adelaide, but Jonathan kept hitching between the two cities—Sydney and Adelaide—and he would disappear for a few weeks at a time.

Looking back, I'm not sure how any of us survived this time. I was still having to work—for financial reasons—at the ABC, writing and interviewing for a three-part documentary series called *A Matter of Chance*, which was about people coping with disabilities (which won a Logie for Best Documentary Series). At the same time, I was travelling like a yo-yo between Adelaide and Sydney. Jonathan's illness was growing ever more severe, and I would try and visit Sydney every couple of weeks, first to find Jonathan—who was frequently in jail—and then to visit

Ellis—who was dying of cancer in Sydney Hospital, not long after he had happily remarried.

Sometimes when Jonathan was psychotic, and it was the middle of the night, he would think I was the devil and his voices were telling him to kill me. I would hold up a large silver Ethiopian cross and tell him, 'No, I am your mother. I love you, and I come in peace.'

Once, after I had just become Chair of the South Australian Film Corporation, and was giving a press conference, Jonathan climbed through a window, naked except for a towel draped round his waist, and with paper clips dangling from his ears. I introduced him and he bowed politely from the waist down, before leaving the room, talking to himself. Because of Jonathan's occasional rages, it was safer for my other son Joshua to go to school as a weekly boarder and for Georgia to stay with the family of a friend.

When he was just twenty-four, Jonathan died in Sydney of an overdose of cheap wine and sedatives. Did he die from the overdose, or die from neglect as months and years passed while I vainly tried to get him help? The day before he died, he had wept in my arms, saying he was too sick to go on living.

Nowadays, there have been major improvements in health systems around Australia and in our understanding of the illness. Many people helped during this period of ignorance and neglect. For several years I was deeply involved in setting up Schizophrenia Fellowships and a national organisation known as SANE AUSTRALIA. I became a member of the New South Wales Mental Health Tribunal. I wrote a book about our life with Jonathan, called *Tell Me I'm Here*, which won a human rights award, and has been published throughout the world—most recently in pharsi in Iran. I also made a one-hour television documentary, called *Spinning Out*, about people living with schizophrenia; and for three or four years I lectured and ran workshops about schizophrenia in Australia, the United States and England. The stigma attached to mental illness was so great that I wanted to help people speak aloud about mental illness and mental health.

The main reason for such prolific work was my determination that schizophrenia should cease to be a mystery; that we should start talking about people who had learned to live with the illness, whose resilience had pulled them through.

II

Seeking Peace

9

Missing Peace

Sydney, December 1999

FAREWELL TO THE MURDEROUS CENTURY

It is the eve of the new millennium in Sydney and I join friends in gazing down at a city bursting with celebration. Crowds thronging streets. Families in parks. The Opera House and the Harbour Bridge ablaze with lights. Boats of every kind and size bob tipsily up and down. At midnight, cascades of pink and yellow fireworks illuminate Sydney Harbour Bridge with the word 'Eternity'. People cheer as they farewell one of the most murderous centuries in recorded history, one in which there was scarcely a corner of the world where we had not killed and maimed each other in various ways, from nuclear weapons to the crudeness of machetes and the sophistication of 'precision bombing' which frequently fails to be precise. I rest my arms on the black iron balustrade of a balcony, so high and distant from the yelling crowds. They seem so vulnerable. All of us seem so vulnerable.

I thought about vulnerability in the months that followed. I was preparing a submission to the ABC for a three-part television series called *War and Peace,* in which I wanted to explore what chance we had of making the next century more peaceful than the one we had just left behind. I had started this work with my partner, Robert Theobald, a tall rangy Englishman who had lived most of his life in America and who had written widely about peace, particularly his belief that one of our challenges was to understand the danger of conflict early: to prevent developments reaching the point where violence was inevitable. We had planned to attend a major London conference on war and peace in July 2000, but Robert died suddenly of an aggressive oesophageal cancer, and for a while I felt too battered to continue. Eventually, I decided to go to London on my own.

London, July 2000

WHAT HAPPENED TO PEACE?

The morning of the conference was damp and cold. When I emerged, blinking, from the darkness of the Underground I noticed that most people seemed to be carrying umbrellas that, in spite of the drizzle, remained firmly closed. Everyone scurried, faces turned towards the ground. As I looked around, I remembered that this part of London was heavily bombed during the Blitz. I thought of the devastation of other cities, the firebombing of Dresden and Cologne, back to the sacking of Troy, only there wasn't time to go back as far as Troy because I was approaching London University's Bedford College, where a large gathering of damp people had assembled to hear one of the world's most eminent war historians, Professor Sir Michael Howard, Yale and Oxford, General of the Grenadier Guards, Military Cross, Fellow of All Souls.

The man who introduced Howard observed that he brought to his audience a felicitous conjunction of arms and letters, and that he wrote with rare insight about some of humanity's most inhumane acts. Howard had a large balding head, highly polished shoes, socks that were firmly in place and an engaging manner. He spoke with ease and energy, giving an elegant, disturbing address that, to me, seemed mainly concerned with the inevitability of war and the fact that conflict is a natural state at every level of human life. He said that war equals energy. It shows us we are not decaying. We have to learn how to make peace virile. Peace was a natural consequence of the growth of economic stability but only becomes possible if conflicts can be subsumed and managed. This requires structures, organisations, laws, time and hard work. At the end—almost as a throwaway line—he observed that men become restless without the excitement of war. Any minute, I thought, dear God, any minute and he will proclaim, 'Once more unto the breach, dear friends, once more . . .'

The conference lasted three days; during that time, in spite of the word 'peace' being part of the conference title, most of the speakers took war as their primary focus. I was curious to discover if the same imbalance occurred in publishers' reading lists, which were on display and the titles for sale. But I hovered so long in trying to count titles that an angular woman in a brown and green cardigan looked at me with frosty suspicion.

Oxford University Press offered only three titles on peace compared with 111 on wars that covered everything from the Viking warriors to the Zulu War, the Charge of the Light Brigade, Pearl Harbor, Stormtroopers, and the Marine Corps in Vietnam.

I still remember my dismay at the end of that first day. What had happened to peace? Why did I feel as if beneath the scholarly debate lay many of the same tired old assumptions about war and its inevitability? I wondered what hubris allows us to believe that war, not peace, is the norm; that man is naturally aggressive and that patterns which have been accepted since earliest times will never change?

'For after grete war cometh good pees/And after the rayne cometh the fair weder,' reads 'The Hares and the Frogs' in the Caxton edition of *Aesop's Fables* (1484). But why, nearly six hundred years later, do we still think of peace as the resolution of war, not as the way to prevent war?

Rain clung to the leaves of trees and water ran down my neck as I walked to the Underground. I swiped at a low-lying branch of a plane tree, frustrated by the realisation that if we continue to present war as sexy and inevitable, and peace as boring and unlikely, we will be unable to move outside a rigidity of thinking that has dominated cultures and behaviour for centuries but whose price is too high to pay at this stage of our social evolution. We are behaving like cavemen, except that instead of clubs we bomb our enemies into submission or oblivion.

Understand that I was not underestimating the enormous complexities of war, nor the difficulties of resolving conflict. This is not a naïve proposition. I recognise the extraordinarily strong economic and cultural forces that will continue to drive traditional patterns of behaviour. The power of multinational industries that manipulate political agendas and profit hugely from wars. The spread of armaments by the very governments that promote peace. The entrenchment of military–industrial complexes and the dazzling technology that allows growing numbers of countries to conduct armchair wars. But as long as we regard peace as a postscript to war, peace-building efforts will remain inadequate and compromised. We need a whole shift in consciousness, in the evolution of peace. We need to challenge old men's tales. Conflict may be inevitable, even useful at times. War and violence are not. If everybody colludes in believing that war is the norm, nobody will recognise the imperative of peace.

On that first night after the conference, I visited an old friend in her apartment in St John's Wood—a quiet 1930s building, trees in the full leaf of summer, a glass of wine, a sense of calm and plenitude and a temporarily stifled awareness that in many other parts of the world there was neither peace nor plenty.

Marianne knew about war and persecution. She was ten years old on 9 November 1938, also known as Kristallnacht, or the Night of Broken Glass, a pogrom against Jews in Nazi Germany and Austria. She jumped from the second-floor window of her family home in Berlin when the Nazis entered. They beat up her parents, ransacked their house, and sent her father to a concentration camp. She never saw him again. One year later, she travelled to England with a luggage label around her neck as a Kindertransport child.

Marianne is now in her early eighties, a handsome woman with greying dark hair who sits and listens to my tirade of hope for the future, nodding. When I have finished talking, she rises to her feet. 'Anne, you are right to have hope.' She hesitates. 'I hope you are right.'

September 11

SHOCKING THE WORLD

Just over a year later, on 11 September 2001, two hijacked jetliners flew into the World Trade Center in New York; a third hijacked plane flew into the Pentagon in Washington DC.

I am in Sydney, at home in bed, asleep, when the phone rings and I hear my son Joshua's voice. Urgent. Shocked. 'Turn on your television, Anne, there's an attack on New York.'

The screen flickers, grey and black shadows become images, images dance their way into startling and terrifying pictures. Planes slice through skyscrapers, skyscrapers crumble like wounded giants, people jump out of windows to certain death. They are holding hands: dear God, such is our need for human closeness. Down below, grey concrete dust blankets everyone and everything. Flames and smoke pursue terrified men, women, children who run blindly through the streets. Fast, fast, as fast as they can.

'I love you.' Messages are sent from those who are trapped in buildings, from those in a plane that is hurtling towards a kamikaze crash. 'I love you.'

The death toll exceeds 3000. Trading on Wall Street stops. President George W. Bush vows that America will lead the world to victory over terrorism in a struggle he terms the first war of the twenty-first century. The United States will respond with a sustained military campaign, not a single strike. The State Department warns that governments will be isolated if they tolerate or assist terrorist groups. 'You are either with us or you're with the terrorists,' says the humiliated American president as he pledges to rid the world of evil-doers. 'I believe that my job is to go out and explain to people what's on my mind. That's why I'm having this press conference, see? I'm telling you what's on my mind. And what's on my mind is winning the war on terror.'

In Bush's autobiography, *Decision Points*, he wrote: 'My blood was boiling. We were going to find out who did this and kick their ass.'

On the supposition that the terrorist attacks were masterminded by the militant Islamic group al-Qaeda, whose leader was Osama bin Laden, a US-led coalition bombed and invaded Afghanistan on 7 October 2001. The war was known as Operation Enduring Freedom and its goal was to dismantle the al-Qaeda terrorist organisation as well as the extremist fundamentalist group the Taliban, which supported and protected al-Qaeda.

Bin Laden was captured and killed in Pakistan on 2 May 2011 but the Taliban remain at large. Eleven years on from September 11, coalition forces are still fighting in Afghanistan and the war has expanded into the tribal areas of neighbouring Pakistan. The war in Afghanistan is the United States' longest running war. Thousands of Afghan civilians have been killed, villages pounded to pieces, family gatherings mistakenly bombed. A quarter of all Afghan children die before the age of five. Protests regularly occur in the streets of Kabul, but the killings continue.

Are we winning the hearts and minds of the Afghan people? Afghan president Hamid Karzai obviously thinks not. In an address to the UN General Assembly on 24 September 2008, he said: 'The continuation of civilian casualties can seriously undermine the legitimacy of fighting terrorism and the credibility of the Afghan people's partnership with the international community.'

Karzai is right to talk about civilian casualties, but this is what happens in war. Innocent people die, soldiers die, children die, infants die. Animals, birds, fish die. The earth dies.

Wars kill, full stop.

Afghanistan is one of the world's most dangerous countries. Assassinations and suicide bombings are common; tribal warfare persists. Because of the country's strategic importance as a focal point of the ancient Silk Road and as a gateway to India, it has been invaded and conquered over many centuries. The prize: access to oil and narcotics. Rich pickings, at a heavy price.

19 March 2003

INVASION OF IRAQ

After reducing Afghanistan to dust and despair, Bush then turned his attention to Iraq on the pretext that its leader, Saddam Hussein, was harbouring weapons of mass destruction. All through that summer of 2002 to 2003 in Australia, the inevitability of going to war with Iraq grew, day after day. Night after night, I found myself obsessed with watching the news. Vast stretches of pale windswept desert. Armour-plated tanks lumbering over the sand. Bombs about to drop from the skies.

Responses to threats of war with Iraq, and to the war itself, were immediate. According to French academic Dominique Reynié, between 3 January and 12 April 2003, 36 million people across the globe protested against the likelihood of war. The strength and size of the demonstrations led *New York Times* journalist Patrick Tyler to claim there were two superpowers on the planet: the United States and worldwide public opinion. So here I am, in Sydney, marching twenty abreast in the pouring rain, about to join a number of other speakers outside Parliament House. We are in the front line, shuffling as we attempt to stop a long printed banner from trailing in the mud. Behind me a small child bangs a saucepan. A few days earlier I had spoken in the coal-mining city of Wollongong to a crowd of mainly miners and Islamic families, some linking arms, some singing, some waving banners. In both places, my horror at the thought of war made me feel the surprising energy of peace.

A large march in Melbourne is soon to come. Marches all over the world. In Rome, three million marched, and the demonstration is now listed in the *Guinness World Records* as the largest ever anti-war rally. Could these marches achieve anything? Why were they happening, given that most of the millions who joined in probably had little knowledge of Iraq or of Islam, and represented so many different ages, races, and political and religious persuasions? Why were we gathering in cities and towns across the world, armed with placards and banners, shouting and chanting our protests? Among the protestors were two of my former neighbours, a conservative couple in their eighties who had never 'done anything like this before' but who deeply disapproved of President Bush exercising pre-emptive rights and believed he was making the world a more dangerous place. Almost certainly there was a mix of reasons for the protests, including anti-American sentiment, but there were also strongly expressed views that war was no way to resolve conflict, and that violent initiatives usually resulted in violent outcomes.

One of the most moving responses to the threat of war came from a group of women in rural New South Wales in a newspaper that was handed to me at a demonstration, with one page of letters to the editor and no title:

> We do not want the drought to be stopped by our tears, we do not want Iraqi children and innocent women and men to suffer at our hands. They have suffered enough already. We do not want to be lied to any more. We do not want dishonour and shame on our country. We do not want to send our service men and women to die in a war that is not of our concern. We want peace with honour.

On 19 March 2003, Iraq exploded into war. Operation Iraqi Liberation was launched with an incendiary shower of cruise missiles, raining down on the heads of frightened Iraqi civilians. Operation Iraqi Liberation became Operation Iraqi Freedom, and Operation Iraqi Freedom became Operation War Against Terror. In this climate, fear soon became a means of fanning support for the war. Fear of jihad. Fear of rogue nuclear attacks. Fear of chemical and germ warfare. Fear of economic policies that already condemned half the world to poverty and disease.

The Great Depression had reached its zenith when Franklin D. Roosevelt beat Herbert Hoover in the 1932 US presidential election. In his inaugural address of 4 March 1933, Roosevelt uttered his now-famous line: 'The only thing we have to fear is fear itself—nameless, unreasoning, unjustified terror which paralyzes needed efforts to convert retreat into advance.'

This clarified for me the full import of fear, and of how in a climate of fear people are easily lulled into silence, easily coaxed into confessions, easily persuaded into accepting the obscenities of war.

Nobel Prize-winner Akinwande Oluwole 'Wole' Soyinka called his 1994 BBC Reith Lectures *Climate of Fear*. He talked about 'the world being sentenced to life imprisonment behind the bars of fear'.

I have another memory—of turning on the television one dreary winter's day when a close-up of George W. Bush jerked into focus. George W. Bush in full military uniform: epaulettes, gold braid, brass buttons, medals. 'I am your War President,' announced the world's new War President, after ordering thousands of missiles to devastate the unsuspecting people of Iraq, even though they had nothing to do with 9/11, nor with weapons of mass destruction. The American bombing mission was named 'Shock and Awe'. I wondered at the shock and awe that might happen if a leader one day said, 'I am your Peace President.'

During the Sydney Writers' Festival in 2003, I spoke at a public forum on 'America, Iraq and the Future of Conflict'. It was raining again but warm and muggy so that a smell of damp inertia once again seemed to permeate the air. The hall of the Seymour Centre was filled to capacity, but the audience was passive, maybe because most people were still shocked at the outcome of America's invasion of Iraq. Most of the discussion was about war. This was hardly surprising, given the slant of the title.

In the end, I jumped up in exasperation. 'Instead of talking about "America, Iraq and the Future of War", why aren't we talking about "America, Iraq and the Future of Peace"? What are the consequences of US actions? Are they likely to help peace or to hinder it?'

There was silence, until a man in the audience, wearing a jacket and a blue checked shirt, creaked to his feet and began applauding. The sound of his two hands clapping reverberated in the hall. When he stopped and sat down, we resumed talking about war.

10

So Why War?

Sydney, 2001

COMPLEXITIES OF WAR

Today is a summer day in Sydney, many years since I was a child of ten standing in a London street, watching a straggle of young soldiers marching off to war. Then it was late autumn and cold, but this morning will be hot, even though an early sea breeze is sending clouds racing across the sky like greyhounds. I am working outside, pruning grapevines that tumble over the iron roof of an old shed, when I notice the spiders have been busy.

All around me, golden webs are swaying in the breeze, stretching from one bush to another, swinging from branches and twigs, doorframes and tables, each one bearing spiders of different kinds and colours: golden orb weavers with silvery-grey bodies and bold yellow stripes down their legs that remind me of rugger players; St Andrew's Cross spiders with ribbons of bluish-white silk that form a cross through the centre of their webs (I call them 'ambulance drivers', except these ambulance drivers don't save their captives, they eat them).

I sit on a nearby wooden bench and watch them for a while. Spiders engaged in the ritual of spinning, killing, eating, dying. There is something about their relentless activity that reminds me of humans preparing for war—although humans rarely eat their captives—and I find myself pondering a question that has been asked over the centuries by some of the greatest thinkers in the world: Why do humans fight wars?

I rise slowly and go into the house to make a cup of coffee, stumbling over the doorstop, my eyes narrowing as I move from sunlight into dark. Take a war, I tell myself, any war, and think of its complexities. A vast range of political, economic and social factors affect the nature and causes of war, and most of them stem from the reactions and manipulations of governments. Unsatisfactory peace deals in the past that lead to payback wars in the future. Legacies of colonial oppression that make trust hard to win and peace even harder to achieve. Policies that condemn half the world to poverty, fostering resentment and anger. The imposition of free markets across the world, leading to social dislocation on a massive scale. And revolt against oppressive regimes of the kind that occurred during the Arab Spring.

Two very different people believed it was foolish, even ridiculous, to try to analyse the reasons humans go to war. Prussian general Carl von Clausewitz wrote that:

> no theorist, and no commander should bother himself with psychological and philosophical sophistries, even though the rational science of war admits the obvious, but

it omits from its calculations weather, personal proclivities of the generals, political pressures, health, intelligence, technical breakdowns. War is the playground of the incalculable.

Leo Tolstoy, the great Russian author, appears to have agonised for a while before writing a postscript to his epic novel *War and Peace*:

Why do millions of people begin to kill one another? Who told them to do it? It would seem that it was clear to each of them that this could not benefit any of them, but would be worse for them all. Why did they do it? Endless retrospective conjectures can be made, and are made, of the causes of this senseless event, but the immense number of these explanations, and their concurrence in one purpose, only proves that the causes were innumerable and that not one of them deserves to be called the cause.

Later, Tolstoy's approach became more concise. 'In all history there is no war which was not hatched by the governments, the governments alone, independent of the interests of the people, to whom war is always pernicious even when successful.'

—

One thing is certain: young men and women seldom march off to war of their own accord. Wars are manipulated by those in power—usually to gain more power. And it is the lambs that go to the slaughter, rarely the wolves.

In the seventeenth and eighteenth centuries, if the British navy was short of seamen, groups of men known as press gangs would roam the streets, looking for men between the ages of eighteen and forty-five, who were then legally forced into service in the Royal Navy. Often fights broke out as groups tried to defend their friends. Conditions at sea were poor and service was dangerous. Any subordination was punished by flogging or execution. Today, instead of flogging there are inducements such as scholarships and sponsorships, reasonable pay, adventurous lives, promises of glory and, in wartime, hopefully survival or, if unlucky, a bugle call at the end.

Memories of 1945

EINSTEIN, MAN OF PEACE

Almost immediately, a memory stirs—one that shifts the discussion away from waging war onto waging peace. Peace with justice. It's a story that, for me, began one cold winter's afternoon in a science laboratory at Sheffield High School in the north of England. The year was 1945. Fog stifled the windows, radiators clanked, girls giggled. Bunsen burners were lined up on ancient wooden benches, waiting to create their alchemy in test tubes filled with pale green liquid: *bubble, bubble, toil and trouble.* A faint smell of hydrogen sulphide wafted through the room—left over from the sixth formers, I decided, wrinkling my nose with disgust at the stink of rotten eggs.

Twenty well-scrubbed girls in brown box-pleat tunics, black wool stockings and black lace-up shoes sat in lines, mouths half open in anticipation, peering at small globules of quicksilver that darted from one end of Petri dishes to the other. At the front of the room was our science teacher, Miss Winifred Stoppard: short, stout and animated.

'Watch the mercury, girls. Joining together then slipping apart. Like Romeo and Juliet and most young love.' She smiled benignly at us, trying to tuck her greying hair into an unruly bun. 'But, girls, wait till you've left school before you find out about young love.'

'Oh Romeo, Romeo, wherefore art thou?' we called to each other, smirking.

Miss Stoppard was one of those rare and passionate teachers who was capable of branching into discussions about the poetry of Walt Whitman in the middle of a lesson about the chemical properties of hydrogen sulphide. Today she had started talking about the properties of mercury and was about to segue into the politics of war. 'Use your brains, girls. None of this stiff upper lip, that's male stuff and so hard for those poor soldiers in the last war when they weren't even allowed to admit they were afraid.'

There was a rumour that Miss Stoppard had had a younger brother who was killed flying over Germany at the end of the Second World War, which was maybe why she returned so frequently to the subject of war. Today she was passing around postcards of a man with a prickly grey moustache and hair like a tangle of garden wire.

'Girls, you are looking at a picture of a good and brilliant man: Dr Albert Einstein, winner of the Nobel Prize for Physics, who spent his life working for human rights and for peace. Not an alchemist, but a scientific genius whose insights were so revolutionary that they challenged established scientific doctrine and altered the way people saw their world.'

She told us that Einstein was born on 14 March 1879 into a liberal, secular and bourgeois German Jewish family. After finishing university he worked as a patent clerk in Switzerland, and in his spare time he began writing scientific papers that altered the way people saw their world. In 1905, when he was only twenty-six, he sent three of these papers to the premier German scientific journal, *Annalen der Physik*. 'To be published if there is room,' he said modestly in a covering note.

$E=mc^2$, Miss Stoppard wrote on the blackboard, white chalk squeaking, our teeth bleating—at least that's how it felt to me. She stepped back, looked at her work, then stood on tiptoe to write at the top of the board: *BLAZING ROCKETS*. When she turned around, her face was flushed and her eyes sparkled. '"Blazing rockets which in the dark of the night suddenly cast a brief but powerful illumination over an immense unknown region." That's how French physicist Louis de Broglie described Einstein's discoveries.'

No wonder I remember the phrase, no wonder I found science so exciting. Biology, physics and chemistry, pure maths and applied maths, I soared with them all. Yet later I dropped them one by one and walked away into a world of ideas and imagination, forgetting that science also required ideas and imagination.

'The release of atom power has changed everything except our way of thinking—the solution to this problem lies in the heart of mankind. If only I had known, I should have become a watchmaker,' said Einstein, probably drawing deeply on his meerschaum pipe, long and curved, made of cherry wood.

Or was it Miss Stoppard who said that? In my mind I have them dancing a polka, round and round they go, frenzy and energy mounting. Winifred Stoppard's hair flies away from the imprisonment of her bun, her brown cardigan bobs up and down. But Miss Stoppard is already spoken for. She lives with our English teacher, who fills our classroom with her thick body and sarcastic tongue. She has a face like a frog. I love Miss Stoppard but I hate Miss Whatsername.

'And so science is exciting because everything and anything is possible,' Miss Stoppard said to us. 'Pathways lead in all directions. Be bold and brave in your journeys. He was.'

'Who?' said a deliberately obtuse girl with braces on her teeth and a red nose. 'Who was bold and brave?'

'Einstein,' we all shouted as the story continued.

When I look back on those days with Miss Stoppard, I recall my exhilaration as the story of Einstein unfurled. To this day, Einstein's genius as a scientist remains unquestioned, but his global championship of human rights and his lifelong commitment to pacifism are not so well known.

Long before 1921, the year he won the Nobel Prize for Physics, Einstein was becoming increasingly outspoken in his political views. He backed organisations that were seeking to protect Jews from anti-Semitic violence, and he openly criticised the German government's growing support of the Nazi party.

Biographer John Simon has noted that Einstein's egalitarian streak led him to offer free after-hours physics classes to poor students who couldn't afford the rising cost of university fees. He used scientific conferences as platforms to address political questions so that he might discuss relativity in the morning and that very evening, urge young people to refuse military service. And in the turbulent aftermath of the First World War, he would take his students to anti-Nazi demonstrations. But first, he would hastily slap notices on his classroom doors: CLASS CANCELLED—REVOLUTION.

'This was very brave of Einstein,' said Miss Stoppard. 'He risked his career. He risked his life.'

And now, for a second, my memory becomes blurred. One of the girls had opened a window and fog billowed into the room, making us cough. Miss Stoppard didn't cough. She leaned on her desk, waving her blackboard pointer as if she were conducting an orchestra.

One summer's day in July 1932, a year before Hitler withdrew Germany from the League of Nations, Dr Albert Einstein sat down in his summerhouse in a quiet little village near Potsdam, in Germany, and wrote an extraordinary letter to Professor Sigmund Freud—'an extraordinary letter, girls':

Dear Professor Freud, This is the problem: Is there any way of delivering mankind from the menace of war? It is common knowledge that, with the advance of modern science, this issue has come to mean a matter of life and death for Civilisation, as we know it. Nevertheless, for all the zeal displayed, every attempt at its solution has ended in a lamentable breakdown.

While Einstein had been busy annoying the Nazis and inspiring his students, the International Institute of Intellectual Cooperation in Paris had just invited him to engage any person of his choice in a frank exchange of views, on any problem he might select. Einstein had chosen war and, as his colleague, the celebrated Austrian psychoanalyst, Professor Sigmund Freud. Both men were Jewish, and both had been alarmed by the rise of Nazism. As tensions increased politically, Einstein's views sharpened. On 20 April 1932 he had already submitted to the Russian-language journal *Nord-Ost* a contribution to a symposium on 'Europe and the Coming War'. He argued that:

> As long as all international conflicts are not subject to arbitration and the enforcement of decisions arrived at by arbitration is not guaranteed, and as long as war production is not prohibited, we may be sure that war will follow upon war. Unless our civilisation achieves the moral strength to overcome this evil it is bound to share the fate of former civilisations: decline and decay.

And then doubt crept into Einstein's thinking. He wrote that he had 'no insight into the dark places of human will and feeling' and hoped that Freud would give him advice outside the scope of politics.

'Here lies, perhaps, the crux of all the complex factors we are considering, an enigma that only an expert in the lore of human instincts can resolve. And so we come to our last question,' wrote Einstein.

> Is it possible to control man's mental evolution so as to make him proof against the psychoses of hate and destructiveness? Here I am thinking by no means only of the so-called uncultured masses. Experience proves that it is rather the so-called 'intelligentsia' that is most apt to yield to these disastrous collective suggestions, since the intellectual has

no direct contact with life in the raw but encounters it in its easiest form—upon the printed page.

Freud replied from his house in Vienna two months later, in September 1932. What did he think when he read Einstein's letter? It can't have come as a complete surprise—after all, the two men had already been corresponding—but the enormity of Einstein's question did seem to take him aback, this elegantly groomed and white-bearded man of seventy-six whose cluster of theories about the unconscious mind, to which was given the name psychoanalysis, had long attracted confrontation and argument.

I like to think of him drawing on one of his finest cigars as he stood in front of a couch he used for psychoanalysis. I squint at a photograph of the couch and see that it appears to be covered in a faded dark red tapestry of Middle Eastern design. One end is a little rumpled.

Dear Mr Einstein,

The question that you put to me—what is to be done to rid mankind of the war menaces?—took me by surprise. And, next, I was dumbfounded by the thought of my (of our, I almost wrote) incompetence; for this struck me as being a matter of practical politics, the statesman's proper study. But then I realised that you did not raise the question in your capacity of scientist or physicist, but as a lover of his fellow men, who responded to the call of the League of Nations much as Fridtjof Nansen, the polar explorer, took on himself the task of succouring homeless and starving victims of the World War.

When Freud responded to Einstein's question about the possibility of controlling man's mental evolution, he wrote about the struggle between Eros and Thanatos, between the instinct of life and the instinct of destruction. He wondered how long we would have to wait before the rest of men became pacifist.

Impossible to say, and yet perhaps our hope that these two factors—man's cultural disposition and a well-founded dread of the form that future wars will take—may serve to put an end to war in the near future, is not chimer-ical . . . Meanwhile we may rest on the assurance that whatever makes for cultural development is working also against war.

The Einstein–Freud exchange was published in three languages under the title *Why War?* and distributed throughout Western Europe at the end of 1932—with the exception of Germany, where it was banned. On 30 January 1933, when the Nazis seized power, the books and papers of both Einstein and Freud were seized and publicly burned. Freud observed drily: 'What progress we are making. In the Middle Ages they would have just burned me. Now they are content with burning my books.' Hitler eventually drove both men into exile, and the Einstein–Freud letters never achieved the wide circulation that was intended.

—

In 1939 and 1940, Einstein wrote to President Roosevelt pointing out the power of the atomic bomb and the danger of its development by Germany. This led to the building and testing of America's first atomic bomb in 1945, and the decision to drop it on Hiroshima three weeks later.

'Doctor,' said a journalist who had walked among the small black bundles that stick to the streets and bridges of Hiroshima, 'Doctor, a human being who has been roasted becomes quite small, doesn't he?'

Einstein protested at the incineration of Hiroshima and Nagasaki, and went on to chair the Emergency Committee of Atomic Scientists (ECAS), whose aim was to remove atomic development from the military and place it under international control.

Einstein was also a long-time anti-racist, and denounced every outrage he witnessed in the US, having seen similar scenes in Germany. In 1946, during a spate of lynchings, civil rights activist, actor and singer Paul Robeson invited Einstein, his lifelong friend, to be co-chair of the American Crusade to End Lynching. Robeson wrote to President Truman, calling for the prosecution of lynchers, the passage of a federal anti-lynching law and the ousting of a racist Mississippi senator, Theodore Bilbo.

The letter was delivered by Robeson, but the meeting was terminated by Truman when Robeson told him that if the government would not protect blacks, they would have to protect themselves. Uproar followed, but Einstein agreed with Robeson. 'There is always a way to overcome legal obstacles whenever there is an inflexible will at work in the service of a just cause.'

Einstein was also concerned about the crises of European Jewry following the Nazi genocide. He helped raise funds for the establishment of Jewish settlements in Palestine, but he was aware of the dangers of oppressive nationalism. 'I can see a future for Palestine only on the basis of peaceful cooperation between the two peoples who are at home in the country . . . come together they must in spite of all.'

—

Einstein was a radical from his student days until his dying breath. Days before he died, on 18 April 1955, Einstein signed what became known as the Einstein–Russell Manifesto, in which he and the great philosopher mathematician Bertrand Russell went beyond vague moral arguments for peace:

> There lies before us, if we choose, continual progress in happiness, knowledge, and wisdom. Shall we, instead, choose death, because we cannot forget our quarrels? We appeal as human beings to human beings: Remember your humanity, and forget the rest. If you can do so, the way lies open to a new Paradise; if you cannot, there lies before you the risk of universal death.

In the last years of his life, while he was ruminating about the political affairs of the day, Einstein told a friend that he remained a 'revolutionary' and was still a 'fire-belching Vesuvius'. 'I do not know how the Third World War will be fought,' he said, 'but I can tell you what we will use in the Fourth—rocks!'

11

War's Just Human Nature

Phuket, Thailand, March 2010

WE CAN'T HELP IT

'Always have wars—in our genes, in our blood,' says a chorus of men one evening, sitting outdoors in the soft night air of Thailand. I don't suppose they did speak as a chorus, but this is how I remember them. Frangipani flowers drop onto our shoulders and the table. I hold one in my hand, enjoying its creamy fragrance and the beauty of its orange centre.

The year is 2010, and I am a guest at a quiet and secluded place somewhere in Phuket, a place of such tranquil beauty that it is hard to imagine wars or violence are remotely possible—not just here but anywhere. Bamboo-thatched villas cluster around a gentle hillside; fountains splash; white-canopied beach buggies come at the touch of a bell; the table in front of us contains the finest yet simplest of delicacies—prawns, mussels and oysters, deep purple beetroot sliced into elegant fans, sprays of pale green shallots, the enticing smell of coriander and lemon.

This soft early evening is the last of our stay and we are gathered around a long table, having drinks before we walk a few paces up stone steps and along a garden path to reach our own private dining pavilion. Everything is catered for. Any tension we might have had when we arrived drifted away almost immediately.

And then it happens. Someone—one of the men—genially asks me what I am writing. I hesitate. I find it difficult to talk about my work until it is finished, but I manage to mumble that I am working on a book about war and peace, with apologies to Tolstoy.

Theories about war range over all of human history: that man is territorial and aggressive by nature, a natural-born killer; that wars are fought because we cannot help it; that wars are normal, have been and always will be. Such theories are usually proposed by men—men from all backgrounds—and they say much the same thing: 'Always have wars—in our genes, in our blood, in our upbringing,' says the admiral, the general, the judge and the stockbroker. 'Always wars,' says the bank manager, the butcher and the garbage collector. 'Good for business,' says the financial consultant, gazing at his computer screen. 'Interest rates up, up, up; health costs up, up, up; new drugs for post-traumatic stress disorder—take 'em myself.'

—

Some weeks later, on Anzac Day, I am at a cafe in Kings Cross telling a lawyer friend that I have just read a newspaper interview with one of Australia's most highly regarded soldiers, General Peter Cosgrove. Cosgrove had said, 'There will always be wars in the world as long as man, the perfect predator, is the dominant species.'

My friend laughs and takes a sip of his coffee. 'Most predators I've encountered end up in jail,' he says, opening his copy of the *Financial Review*.

The pages flutter like a pile of banknotes in the early morning breeze. I glance at a headline and wish I hadn't:

AMERICANS BOMB WEDDING PARTY IN AFGHANISTAN. TEN CHILDREN DEAD. A REGRETTABLE MISTAKE SAYS US GENERAL

'Fuckin' hell, no more bloody wars,' says a voice behind me. A hoarse old man's voice, a voice that creaks its way into our conversation uninvited, the voice of a body in a wheelchair, a legless torso covered in a tartan blanket, a torso with medals pinned from one armpit to the other, a ghost from a newspaper story—where does this voice come from: this angry old man with the rheumy eyes?

The glory of war makes no sense to people who have been there. I have yet to see a war vets' parade in which soldier after soldier, old man after old man, does not condemn the act of war. Old soldiers cry before they fade away.

Across the other side of the world, in England, Harry Patch—aged 111—is also angry. Harry Patch was a reluctant young conscript, eighteen years old in 1917, when he fought in the Battle of Passchendaele at Ypres, France. He still remembers vividly the fear and bewilderment of going 'over the top'.

As the battalion advanced, the mud was crusted with blood and the wounded were crying out for help. 'But we weren't like the Good Samaritan in the Bible, we were the robbers who passed them by and left. It was not worth it, it was not worth one let alone all the millions who died . . . the Germans suffered the same as we did.'

Harry Patch had a cider, Patch's Pride, named after him, an honorary degree from Bristol University and the Legion of Honour from France. He said thank you, and then in the year 2007 he wrote a book called *The Last Fighting Tommy*. The preface reads: 'Politicians who took us to war should have been given guns and told to settle their differences themselves, instead of organising nothing better than legalised mass murder.'

I think of my brother John. If he were still alive he would be an old man in his eighties. But I still remember him as a young pink-faced officer cadet, aged nineteen, about to fly to Somalia and then the Sudan. I feel frustrated. I want to ask him what he felt about war, but John is dead and now it is too late. Why don't we talk about such huge issues more often? How come Messrs Bush, Blair and Howard took our countries to war without so much as a by-your-leave? Were they the perfect predators, or could it be that for thousands of years a legacy of lies and myths have perpetuated and glorified war? Myths that war is the norm, the ground of our being—is now and ever shall be; that man is a killer by nature and wars are a manifestation of human instinct, offering man's finest hour, an opportunity for nobility and glory. Myths that blind us from seeing the realities of war.

KILLER APES

So let's go back many thousands of years and look at very old bones that, in time, became very old fossils and exerted a powerful influence on the way many people still regard war and peace.

Theories about the origins of war range over all of human history, but one that I remember from the sixties was Robert Ardrey's book *African Genesis*, which gave us a picture of a sky-swept savannah, glowing with menace, on which roamed our immediate forebears, 'the killer apes' whose murderous instincts remain deeply ingrained in humans despite a veneer of civility.

'Africa scared me,' wrote Ardrey. The melodramatic argument that he presented as scientific truth did not lie in any credible evidence, but came from Ardrey's own emotions about Africa, when he stated, 'I sampled in the terror-bright streets of Nairobi the primal dreads of a primal continent.'

'Man is the only species that kills its own,' Ardrey declared—a message that was intoned in solemn voices in classrooms around the world; I still remember a wild-eyed scripture teacher with long grey hair and one missing tooth who insisted in my high school years that only God could redeem us from our animal savagery. Contemporary textbooks still contain references to Ardrey, even if refuting his theory that killing is in our genes. According to the killer-ape theory, aggression remains the driving force behind human evolution. War is our destiny. Full stop. Ardrey also stated that acquired characteristics cannot be inherited, which means that no child born today can differ at birth in significant measure from the earliest of Homo sapiens.

As descendants of these bloodthirsty ancestors, we therefore cannot help waging war. Not guilty, Your Honour, of the genocidal killings of one and a half million Armenians, six million Jewish people, nearly one million Rwandans, millions in Darfur and, for centuries, the relentless massacres of indigenous people around the world. War is our destiny. We are born this way and we cannot help it. Once a killer ape, always a killer ape. Pass a banana, please.

I can think of lots of humans who act like killer apes, which is dangerous if they are in high political office, but Ardrey's theories have been largely rejected by anthropologists of the calibre of Richard Leakey, who accord them little more scientific rigor than a *Planet of the Apes* movie. Leakey agrees that while our ancestors appear to have been hunters, there is no suggestion they were any more bloodthirsty than other predators, and no hint they killed each other more than any other animal species known today.

Modern studies of the behaviour of wild animals reveal that many species kill members of their own kind far more frequently than human beings kill each other. Some species have lives filled with violence, but others live in egalitarian communities, with child rearing shared by males and females. In fact, by comparison with most animal species, man is a more peaceable and less aggressive creature, even when the carnage of modern wars is taken into account. Killer-ape arguments also ignore the fact that, for 99 per cent of human history, humans lived in small stable bands of related hunter-gatherers, practising cooperation and being highly egalitarian. Much of biology survives by cooperation and has to: the alternative is death.

One of the most interesting reflections on ape and human behaviour has been written by Robert Sapolsky, a professor of biology, neurology and neurological sciences at Stanford University. Sapolsky asks how humans differ from our ancestors of sixty thousand years ago. Each of us comes into the world as a small being who is much the same as one of those ancestors. The essential transformations that have taken place since then aren't situated in the genetically inherited structure of our organisms. Instead, they reside in the world into which we are born. We end up very differently to our ancestors because we learn not simply knowledge but how it is best applied. Variation in social practices occurs across species. Some have lives filled with violence.

'Some [ape species] kill one another's infants with cold-blooded stratagems worthy of Richard III,' says Sapolsky. 'Some use their tool-making skills to fashion bigger and better cudgels . . . [And some] engage in what can only be called warfare. Organised proactive group violence.'

Patterns relate to environment. Less aggressive species, such as gibbons or marmosets, live in lush rainforests where food is plentiful and life is easy. Couples mate for life and males help substantially with childcare. But more violent species, such as baboons and rhesus monkeys, seem to be the opposite, with bad behaviour the norm. It appears that some primate species can be either violent or peaceful, with their behaviour driven by their social structures and ecological setting. The challenge is to figure out under what conditions good behaviour is most likely—for apes and humans alike.

If we look at studies of the chimpanzee, beginning with the influential research of Jane Goodall, we are reminded that chimps are our closest relatives, and that we share an astonishing 98 per cent of our DNA with them. Peaceful? No! Not the chimps. Goodall and others have carefully documented an endless stream of murders, cannibalism and organised group violence among their subjects. The evolutionary fate of humans might thus seem preordained by the excesses of these first cousins.

But along comes another chimpanzee species, traditionally ignored because of its small numbers, its habitat in remote rainforests and the fact that its early chroniclers published their findings in Japanese. These new chimpanzees are skinny little creatures originally called pygmy chimps, now known as bonobos, recognised as a separate and distinct species that is just as closely related to humans as the standard-model chimp.

'And boy, is this ever a different ape,' says Sapolsky. Bonobos respect hierarchies, they are able to resolve conflict, yet they are also social, share food, share sex, share everything, and are so different from their cousins the chimps that it's perfectly acceptable to say chimps are from Mars, bonobos are from Venus. Bonobos also have well-developed means of reconciling social tensions: sex in every conceivable position.

Baboons are another question and an unlikely breeding ground for pacifists. They go in for chest thumping, and the ones that need to use it are often about to lose it. Alpha males search out alpha females, yet a female can sneak away from a male that beats her up in favour of one that builds friendly relations with females, helps take care of the kids, goes in for grooming his mate, and can avoid the burnout and injuries of the gladiator apes. Clearly we have as much in common with violent species as the gentle ones. Some species are violent, some peaceful. Just as with primates, human behaviour is often driven by what is happening in our lives and in our ecological settings.

Empathy is the glue that holds human society together, and if humans are empathetic animals it is because we have the backing of a long evolutionary history—as have monkeys, cetaceans, elephants and rodents. All are able to exhibit empathy and moral intelligence.

I think of villagers in Northern Ireland, going out at night in freezing cold weather to try to rescue a pod of whales; of whole communities coming together after the 2010 oil spill in the Gulf of Mexico and working to free birds and sea life from the black sticky oil. And I recall photographs taken during the devastating floods in Queensland in 2011, when small boats rescued not just men, women and children, but dogs, kangaroos and even snakes.

Dutch biologist Frans de Waal, named as one of *Time Magazine*'s hundred most influential people in 2007, has undertaken lengthy research into the innate capacity for empathy that exists among primates. His work has led him to believe that humans and non-human great apes are simply different types of apes, and that empathetic and cooperative tendencies are continuous between these species. 'We need to build on that—to develop these positive tendencies and not the warlike ones, nor the ones that are just concerned with competition,' he says.

The world was not like this when I was growing up. Our empathy often did not extend to animals. Yes, pets and working animals were valued, but they could also be cruelly treated without any repercussions. The idea of birds communicating, or elephants mourning the death of one of their kind, or dolphins coming to the rescue of drowning swimmers, would have been brushed aside as ridiculous.

ALL THAT TESTOSTERONE

And yet a cloud of biological pessimism lingers. This time it shifts from ape ancestors to testosterone, the male hormone that underlies aggression. I am walking on the beach four hours south of Sydney at a place called Guerilla Bay. Dark clouds are chasing away the early-morning sun, dead gulls lie crumpled on the sand, an oystercatcher—a bird with black plumage, a handsome long red beak and elegant dark pink legs—stalks the shallows looking for food. Bluebottles lie scattered on the sand like intricate pieces of blown glass. When I tread on one, it explodes with a loud pop. It reminds me of those little yellow aid packs that the US dropped over Afghanistan, a great idea except they were identical to little yellow landmines that children kept picking up, unaware they were dangerous.

I keep noticing how often my mind returns to war and realise this is one of the problems with writing about peace. The phrase 'war and peace' seems to balance so easily on the tongue, yet there is an asymmetry. War usually swallows peace. So why do I persist in this firm belief that in the last one hundred years or so, the world has been undergoing a shift in consciousness away from war? I am not being naïve. I am not saying that if only we love each other there will be no more wars. But I still believe our attitudes are changing—slowly, like an inchworm moving across booby-trapped terrain. Perhaps this is hard to believe, after the horrors of ethnic cleansing in Serbia, Croatia and Bosnia, and then in Rwanda. Or the indiscriminate killing of civilians in Syria. But as UK writer and broadcaster William Shawcross points out, ethnic cleansing also happened on a vast and horrible scale at the breakup of the Ottoman Empire in the early twentieth century when there was no international community to do anything about it. 'Now there is,' observes Shawcross, 'and with fits and starts, this community is making progress.'

'William Shawcross, are you sure?' I mutter. The notion that we might have obligations to human beings beyond our borders simply because we belong to the same species is a recent invention, and its reach grows longer and longer.

I am so deep in thought that I nearly run into an elderly couple strolling hand in hand on the beach. They are Buddhists and live on the cliff top in a modest house nestling into yellow flowering banksias and eucalypts with trunks of white scribbly bark. Brightly coloured parrots zoom in and out of the silvery foliage that rises high above this small semicircle of beach and rock. Their house is surrounded by trees and hidden from view, unlike the new and very large pavilion house that dominates the entire headland. They ask what I am writing; when I tell them, the man, who has a gentle untroubled face, starts scratching at the sand with his cane. 'Ah,' he says, his face now wrinkling into a despairing frown. 'But what are we to do about men? What about all that aggression, that testosterone?'

His wife adjusts her paisley scarf and nods in agreement. 'All that testosterone,' she repeats.

In fact, a new study challenges the commonly held wisdom that testosterone causes aggression in humans and proposes instead that the hormone encourages status-seeking behaviour.

Research has found that testosterone has a similar effect in rodents. 'Folk wisdom generalizes and adapts these findings to humans, suggesting that testosterone induces antisocial, egoistic or even aggressive human behaviours,' say the authors of the study, published in *Nature*, December 2009.

But research at the universities of Zurich and London shows that the hormone does not have the same effect in humans as it does in animals. 'The preconception that testosterone only causes aggressive or egoistic behaviour in humans is thus clearly refuted,' writes Christoph Eisenegger, a neuroscientist at Cambridge University, who believes the popular wisdom that the hormone causes aggression is deeply entrenched.

'It appears that it is not testosterone itself that induces aggressiveness, but rather the myth surrounding the hormone,' states economist Michael Naef of the University of London.

These studies arguably show that testosterone cannot be cited as a valid explanation for why humans perpetuate war. It reminds me of how men used to be excused for committing rape because they had all that testosterone and couldn't help it. And that women were said to induce rape when they wore their skirts too short and the men couldn't help it. Or, as Sheik Taj Din al-Hilali clearly believed when he was Mufti of Australia, men were seduced into committing rape. Because they couldn't help it. 'If you take out uncovered meat and place it outside on the street, or in the garden or in the park, or in the backyard without a cover, and the cats come and eat it . . . whose fault is it, the cats or the uncovered meat?' he said to 500 worshippers in Sydney during a Ramadan sermon. 'The uncovered meat is the problem. If she was in her room, in her home, in her hijab, no problem would have occurred.'

Mainstream ethnic communities around Australia condemned Sheik al-Hilali's argument, stating firmly that the standard of someone's dress should never be used to justify rape, which is a criminal offence.

12

So What Is Peace?

So what is peace, and where does it lie? In the earth, the sky and the sea, in thunderstorms and tornadoes, in lakes and streams, as a living, breathing presence that balances itself against the weight of war, and which is present but not always seen—here in the hearts of humans and in all of life.

Bondi Beach, February 2002

REBRANDING PEACE

Everything glitters. The sun, the sky, the sea, the oil on sunbathers mown down by the heat of the day. I am thinking, lazily, that war also glitters—its weapons are shiny, sexy, dangerous—when a man with a blond ponytail eases his way into a chair at my table and asks if he can join me. I notice he has large white running shoes, white teeth, and he smiles. He has a good smile. There is just too much of it.

We are strangers, locked behind our sunglasses, when, after a few feeble attempts at small talk—from me as well as from him—he tells me he has just been to the Middle East on a marketing assignment. 'To rebrand Saudi Arabia,' he says eagerly.

I ask him why, what will he do in Saudi Arabia?

'What d'you mean, what will I do?'

'Well, for instance, are you going to do anything about sharia law?'

'Oh, I don't know anything about law. This is a marketing exercise. Aimed at getting more tourists.'

'Then tell them not to steal anything. They might get a hand chopped off.'

He blanches and looks down at his hands. 'But they'd only chop off Arab hands. Not Australian hands.'

There is an awkward silence, and I am about to disappear into my newspaper when he clears his throat and says, 'What about you?'

'What about me?'

'You know, what's your line?'

'I write.'

'What about?'

'Peace.'

He groans. 'One of those.' His bracelet jangles on the white tabletop as he leans forward. 'Writing about peace is like pissing in the wind. Peace isn't going anywhere. It needs a rebrand.'

In a world where everything is branded and rebranded, including wars that are fought in the name of peace, I shouldn't have been so surprised but, for me, branding carries unwelcome connotations—to mark with a brand, to stigmatise, to burn. I look down at my bare arms. Arms were the place where frightened Jewish citizens were often branded and numbered as they entered Nazi concentration camps. Branded by burning, branded by war, branded as a slave, branded for life. To rebrand? From what to what? The man who is rebranding Saudi Arabia has a red alligator branded on his black T-shirt.

So here, in the twenty-first century, gazing across this deep blue ocean, how might I answer a man who tells me that writing about peace needs a rebrand?

'Rebrand white doves,' I suggest. Now it's my turn to be facetious.

He nods, without much enthusiasm.

'Strip 'em naked,' I offer.

He looks alarmed. He finishes his Coke, scrapes back his chair with a metallic noise, and mutters something about a parking ticket. As I watch him jogging down the walkway, I wonder why the word 'peace' rouses such conflicting emotions in people, from the passion of those who risk their liberty or their lives in the name of it, to the cynicism of others, like American journalist and satirist Ambrose Bierce who, in his book *The Devil's Dictionary*, described peace as 'a period of cheating between two periods of fighting'.

As an impatient adolescent who devoured more books than food, my image of peace was that of a boring and worthy aunt who sat on an upright wooden chair in the corner of our kitchen, knitting a scarf that kept unravelling at the bottom as fast as her needles clicked away at the top. The fact that I never had an aunt who knitted was irrelevant to my perception of peace in post-war Europe as a slow and dangerous enterprise. We had just returned to England from living as refugees in Australia, and wherever we went all I could see was the devastation and suffering of war. War was a rampaging dragon that at any moment might flick its tongue and send us all up in flames, including my mysterious aunt.

When I am home and have rubbed the sand from my feet, I pull down the *Concise Oxford English Dictionary* where I find peace defined as:

Freedom from disturbance; tranquillity.
Freedom from or the cessation of war.
A treaty agreeing peace between warring states.

—

I have never believed peace was dependent upon war for its existence. Peace has its own identity, a belief that I found expressed as far back as 1670, when Spinoza, one of the great philosophers of the seventeenth century, wrote: 'Peace is not an absence of war, it is a virtue, a state of mind, a disposition for benevolence, confidence, justice.' I like this definition because it respects the presence of peace in its own right. It recognises its qualities, and it honours the need for justice. Peace is worthless without justice.

Spinoza was a glass grinder, a man who lived quietly and died early—he was only forty-five—but I look at his portrait and feel calmed by its mildness. This was a gentle man, long of face, with lovely dark eyes and a benevolent, inquiring expression. 'I have made a ceaseless effort not to ridicule, not to bewail, not to scorn human actions, but to understand them,' he said.

Three hundred years after Spinoza, Chilean writer Ariel Dorfman, whose country suffered grievously under the tortures of the Pinochet regime, described peace as: 'The deep well of truth of what we all want, each man, each woman, each child on this earth; that the small space that surrounds our fragile bodies be respected, that our right to some minimal territoriality or identity or autonomy be afforded recognition by those who have the power to smash and invade it.'

I read this and shiver. It is night, and I am alone except for my dog, Clodagh, who lies curled up at my feet. She is large and shaggy, with a yellow coat that sheds copious fur, and strangely beautiful yellow eyes that seduced me when I rescued her from a dog pound in outback New South Wales. At the time, I had just finished rereading Doris Lessing's book *The Memoirs of a Survivor*, where anarchy prevails and wandering gangs of feral youths roam the streets, looting and burning. An unnamed woman, and Emily—the child she protects—are guarded by an animal called Hugo, half dog, half cat, who gazes out of a front window with his yellow eyes. Now, I look around me in the silence of my house.

So how else might I describe peace? A state of mind? A state of being? An ideal that motivates human behaviour? A process, painstakingly built? Or something more formal, like the ending of armed conflict between organised political groups? I keep returning to this question because peace has many meanings. For me, it is a way of thinking and being in the world—something that doesn't always come easily to me. And then there are all those other questions: what drives peace, makes peace active? How does an aggressive society or individual become a peaceful one? How can peace thrive when powerful military–industrial complexes are manipulating political agendas and making vast profits from war?

This last question was a hard one to research, because corruption has many tentacles. For example, an explosive article by Jane Mayer in the *New Yorker*, 'Dick Cheney and the Halliburton Controversy', tells how in the run-up to the Iraq war, Halliburton, one of the largest oilfield services corporations, was awarded a US$7.7 billion contract for which—'unusually'— only Halliburton was allowed to bid. Mayer's article explains how Cheney's policies set up Halliburton as one of the few companies able to handle many of the military's outsourcing needs, leading to a huge role in today's military operations. Cheney earned US$44 million from that deal, and retired during the 2000 US presidential campaign with a severance package worth US$36 million.

PROMISE OF PEACE

I am working late. Window shutters are closed and a streetlight shines through the cracks. I hear an occasional car drive past and turn the corner down to the rocks and the sea.

Tonight, I am in search of one of the most interesting philosophers of the Enlightenment, Immanuel Kant (1724–1804), who wrote a text called *Perpetual Peace: A philosophical sketch*. Kant was the son of a saddler who lived in Konigsberg. Portraits show a man with an immensely high forehead, a long pointed nose and a 'no-nonsense' mouth. He was reared in a household that stressed the value of intense religious devotion and a disciplinary education. At the time he wrote *Perpetual Peace* he was seventy-one, experiencing a period when war was regarded as the norm in most people's lives—mind-numbing, perpetual war in a Europe that was still caught in the turbulent aftermath of the French Revolution of 1789.

Kant became one of the first to argue that perpetual peace would one day be achieved, gradually and painfully, as history evolved and we left our adolescence behind. He believed that the species as a whole was making moral progress by embodying moral law through its institutions. Morality was reason internalised. Law was reason externalised. He initially rejected the idea of a world government or federation of nations, deeming this to be despotic, but later envisioned a loose confederation or league of nations, obedient to universal law as a moral cosmopolitanism.

A few days after exploring Kant, I was down at the beach again with the sea surging around my feet, wondering if we would ever reach a peaceful adulthood or if we would blow ourselves up while still in the anger of our adolescence, when a surfer came flying towards me, skimming over the surface. Suddenly he was swallowed by a towering blue wall of water. I held my breath. Miraculously he reappeared, dancing like a circus rider on the white mane of a wave. I shivered with excitement, yet the truth is I have been scared of the sea ever since we first arrived in Australia in 1942.

'Don't be afraid,' my brother John kept telling me the first time we went for a swim in the ocean. 'Don't be afraid,' as he tried to coax me further and further away from the shore while I held back, my mouth firmly closed. I wasn't used to pounding surf and giant waves. Sun glinting on the water, waves rearing up in front of me, plunging me into a terrifying tunnel from which there seemed no escape. Mouth now open, choking, frightened, until I was dumped, breathless, on the shore.

'Good wave,' shouted my brother.

I gave him a withering stare.

Our childhood summers in southern England had merely exposed us to the harmless-looking waves of Brighton Beach. Instead of dumping us, they froze us. We would emerge, shivering and goose-pimpled, and race over the black and white pebbles that were Brighton's offering to tender feet. The pebbles hurt, and on our way back to our towels we would scream to see who could make the loudest noise.

'Don't be such cowards,' my mother's youngest aunt would snap. Aunt Kate was widowed. Her husband had died of a heart attack at Monte Carlo, playing the cards, and left her almost destitute. But she managed to stay on in their old basement apartment in a house in Hove, a suburb next to Brighton. Here, she made a living by reading tarot cards and holding séances in a drawing room draped in heavily fringed Indian shawls. Aunt Kate had a tart voice and a formidably straight back. She said she was the medium to a spirit called Clara who gave her regular instruction in how to calm her inner life and the lives of others.

'I believe firmly in the promise of universal peace,' she would say as she poured a pale and delicate brew of China tea. At some point in the tea-making ceremony she would glare at me. 'Sit up, child. Your posture is abominable.'

It was all very well for elderly Aunt Kate to promote the promise of universal peace, but I never felt quite confident—until I came across a view of peace that made me feel more optimistic.

PEACE: A WAY OF LIFE

In 2000, eminent American Quaker sociologist Dr Elise Boulding wrote a book called *Cultures of Peace: The Hidden Side of History* in which she put forward a woman's view of peace and war, not a man's. It went something like this: throughout history, the missing element in the way we view human experience is an image of the dailiness of life—the common round from dawn to dawn that sustains human existence. Even if battles are raging and bombs are falling, somehow or other we have to get on with the business of life and living. Boulding's view of the common round applies to people of all ages, races and religions. It relates to the small ordinary happenings of life: sharing a meal, playing with children, working at something we enjoy, being with someone we love, being at peace with ourselves—acts of grace that men as well as women are now enjoying much more than when I was a child. These are such fertile and expansive concepts, whose reality ebbs and flows through every part of our lives so that we scarcely notice it, barely think about it, except if our world explodes in conflict or disasters.

And even then, peace usually manages to sneak itself into the midst of tragedy. For a while it is invisible. Then, when the time is right, it fills the air with its presence. It asserts itself as refugees turn black plastic shelters into homes, make a hearth from whatever twigs and stones they can muster, feed their children with whatever food they can find.

In the midst of horrors like the 1994 genocide in Rwanda, when over 800,000 people were slaughtered, I witnessed this driving need to rebuild. On a barren square mile of black rock in neighbouring Zaire, in the lee of a volcano angrily spewing flame and smoke, nearly a million refugees were being sheltered and fed. Bassinets made from twigs hung from poles. Mothers suckled their babies. Children played with toys made from wire and bottle tops. An old man and two children set up a stall and began trading cardamom and ginger, pineapples and bananas. A young boy with a heavy mop of dark hair that fell over his eyes was brandishing a Kalashnikov; he was the only one I avoided. I already knew enough about the recruitment of child soldiers to realise that they had often been so cruelly abused that they found it normal to return cruelty without mercy.

Despite the commonly held view that war is inevitable, there have always been those who felt that humanity could cease its terrible battles. Andrew Bacevich, writing in the *London Review of Books*, suggested that there were two prevailing western views about peace. One view saw war as brutal, capricious, and subject to only precarious control. Force worked, so there was nothing to suggest we would be going out of the war business. The other view was that war was on the way out, and that in the meantime it could be sanitised. Bacevich described well-meaning Europeans as having their heads in the sand, and angry Americans as having blood in their eyes: 'The dynamic depends on history, time, and culture,' he wrote. 'Some societies are civil societies; others are less organized in their government and more prone to violent eruption.'

The longest and costliest war in Australia's history was the Vietnam War, from 1962 to 1972. Initially, public opinion was strongly in support of Australia's involvement in this conflict. Looking back, I think Australians fell for the 'domino theory' promoted by the US government: that if a state fell to communism, the surrounding countries in the region would follow in a domino effect. Atishoo, atishoo, all fall down. But as ever more Australian soldiers were killed in battle, and stories were leaked of atrocities committed against Vietnamese civilians, public protests mounted. In particular, I recall the widespread horror when news broke of the mass murder and mutilation of unarmed civilians in the Vietnamese village of My Lai. Most of the victims were women, children and elderly people.

Since Australia's commitment to the war in Vietnam and the rise in protest movements from 1965, I became politically involved through writing, broadcasting, talking and in protest marches. Conscientious objectors who resisted the call to military service by burning their call-up letters could be, and were, sent to jail. I had a daily radio program on 2GB called *Newsmakers*, dealing with political and social issues, and I invited draft resisters to come to the studio and discuss their views. A lookout was posted on exits and entrances to tip us off if police were on their way. As long as ratings were high, management left me alone.

Then there was the time I met Palestinian human rights lawyer and author Raja Shehadeh. We were both taking part in the 2003 Sydney Writers' Festival, where we shared a stage talking about resilience. Raja is a gentle, thoughtful man with a quick sense of humour, whose need for resilience was challenged in brutal circumstances when in 2002 Ariel Sharon's Israeli government ordered a one-month siege of Ramallah, the administrative centre of Palestinian self-rule and headquarters of Palestinian leader Yasser Arafat. At the time of the siege, Ramallah was Raja Shehadeh's home.

Ramallah lies north of Jerusalem and is a small town of pine trees and old stone buildings with a population of about 50,000. Much of the city was reduced to rubble during the bombardment. Raja kept a diary of the occupation that he later developed into a book, *When the Bulbul Stopped Singing*.

Previously, Raja had worked in New York as a legal expert for Palestinian negotiations on the Oslo Peace Accords, but he became disillusioned by the slowness of negotiations and decided to return to his home. He wanted to write books, listen to music, grow roses and walk in the beautiful hills that surrounded his house.

During the siege his life changed. He wrote about the wanton destruction of houses and public buildings by the Israeli army of occupation. Curfews and rumbling tanks, terrified children, gloved men looking for body parts, a woman shot as she hung out her washing, not enough to eat or drink, a life suspended by fear and, beneath all this, a profound and desperate need to find times of peace, if only for a few precious moments. It was on these occasions that he turned to his diary:

> It has turned out to be a beautiful, sunny first of April day . . . The sun was shining, and for the first time since the invasion the birds were singing in the courtyard. The loudest was the bulbul, a bird with a deep expressive voice whose song sounds like a repetition of the phrase: I told you so, I told you so. The birds were happy because it had rained in the morning. They can take little baths in the puddles. My grandmother used to say, 'Shatwit nisan ibtihi el insan.' (The smell of rain in April revives man.)

The night after meeting Raja, I went with some friends to an Italian restaurant in Surry Hills. We sat outdoors; children were giggling, the question of safety didn't enter our minds, a friend threw a bread stick so the children giggled even more. This same friend—who knew I had been wrestling with this book on peace—observed softly, 'Peace is what is happening in most places most of the time. It's virtually unnoticeable because it is a background to almost everything. A bit like Newton's absolute space.' There was silence. Nobody knew what he meant, or, if they once knew, they had forgotten.

When I got home I looked up Newton and his absolute space: *Abstract space, infinitely extendable, independent of mundane, transient objects.*

Which brought about an interesting reflection: are we perhaps the mundane transient objects, living not in abstract space but in absolute space? Peace is what we live in.

—

The world is not always at war. Wars come and go, yet because of the centrality of war in public consciousness, stories of war dominate our sense of who we are.

Now, in 2012, I am walking along the shoreline, heading to South Bondi, and remembering that this stretch of the beach with its drifts of salt spray from the sea and garlic from the pizza bars was where I last took part in an anti-war demonstration; that was in February 2003, the beginning of the war against Iraq.

Years earlier, in one of the very first marches against the war in Vietnam, I lost my friends in the crowd and fell in with a group of Quakers; they were running and stumbling to keep up with their leader, a vigorous elderly man in brown checked plus-fours who zoomed up and down on roller skates. He was blowing a boy scout's whistle as he tried to shepherd his flock along Macquarie Street and down towards Circular Quay with its old-fashioned ferryboats, the Opera House with its sails about to take flight, and the buskers. I joined the Quakers because I enjoyed their leader's eccentricity and knew of their long history of pacifism.

And then I thought of the bright courage of humanity, unexpected, resolute, and stretching back as far as the history of humankind—people defying oppression and giving their lives for freedom. Marches and demonstrations through the centuries. People enduring torture and dying for justice and for peace. As the Dalai Lama commented: 'Brute force can never subdue the basic human desire for freedom.'

Fragile stuff, you might say, when idealists are pitted against the weight of corporate empires and massive armies, but it is important to ask how, over the centuries, this flame persists. What is it and where does it come from, like a burned tree regenerating with an absurd and magical crown of green?

Peace doesn't need rebranding. It has a spine and sinews, muscles, a brain and a heart. It takes courage and humility to broker peace; patience, a willingness to take risks and, in the words of Spinoza, a capacity to understand opposing points of view.

Wars and violence are not life. They are events, grotesque and brutal. Like Munch's painting *The Scream*, their memory is often beyond words. Peace is not an event. It is a way of life, one that all too readily we take for granted.

AUSTRALIA'S OTHER WARS

I have long been dismayed that among the least acknowledged conflicts in the nation's history were those that ended in the total subjugation of the rights of Australia's indigenous peoples.

The eminent anthropologist, W.E.H. Stanner described the failure of historians to tell of these encounters as 'the great Australian silence'.

It is ironic that despite this silence about the devastation of Aboriginal ways of life, it was the voice of an Aboriginal Australian that protested against the mistreatment of Jews in Europe on the eve of war in 1938. Following the violence of Kristallnacht, when Jewish synagogues, businesses, homes and people were attacked across Germany, it was William Cooper, an elderly Victorian Aboriginal man—ex shearer, drover, horse-breaker—who founded the Australian Aborigines League to empower his own suffering people, and who led a march to the German Consulate in Melbourne to protest against the cruel racism of the Nazi regime.

The world's major holocaust museum in Jerusalem, Yad Vashem, now honours William Cooper's protest with a memorial garden and a research chair worth one million dollars for the study of Holocaust resistance.

Aboriginals say there is no such thing as an Aboriginal problem; the problem is that of white Australians who have successfully deprived them of their land, their culture and their identity. How many times during the Royal Commission on Human Relationships did we hear about their pressing desire for self-determination? It is a common story, told in the pages of history books all over the world.

True improvements will only come about if Aboriginals are allowed to exercise control over their own affairs, to achieve their own successes and failures, and to have the financial resources to make this possible.

—

Anyone with a commitment to peace feels some shame if their own nation wages war more vigorously than peace, and devotes more resources to military force than to its prevention or to reparation of its consequences. It is good to know that Australia has contributed to keeping peace: the Australian War Memorial website records that, since 1947, some 30,000 Australian peace-keepers have taken part in over fifty operations, in more than twenty-four theatres of conflict around the world, as well as a similar number of disaster-relief operations. But Australia's involvements in imperial and then foreign wars, such as in Vietnam, have been highly controversial, not least its military role in Iraq and in Afghanistan, which continues to take the lives of young soldiers as I write. It was when I marched in a huge protest rally against Australia's involvement in the war against Iraq that I determined to write this book.

13

Rights and Relationships

IN LOVE WITH THE WORLD

The first time I went to Paris, I was nineteen and in love with almost everything I saw. When I returned there several years later, I was exploring bookshops and stalls along the banks of the River Seine one Sunday morning when I came upon Simone de Beauvoir's *The Second Sex*. The shop was called Shakespeare & Co. and had been known since the early fifties as a gathering place for writers, including Ernest Hemingway and James Joyce. It was alive with books—books from all over the world, books on shelves, on window ledges, in stacks that were filled with cushions and bedding for any homeless writer who needed somewhere to sleep overnight.

When I saw the owner of the shop, George Whitman, I held out de Beauvoir's book. 'How much?' I asked.

'Give what you can, take what you need,' he said, pointing to a painted sign on one of his walls with the same message.

A few lines of poetry were also painted on the walls: *Be not inhospitable to strangers, lest they be angels in disguise.*

Visiting authors and students were welcome to work and stay at Shakespeare & Co. We could *tap tap* at an old-fashioned typewriter upstairs, or play an old-fashioned piano downstairs.

I often went to George's shop. I made friends there and I used his typewriter to write letters home—sometimes imagining myself as a foreign correspondent writing a column from Paris. One particular morning, as I typed, boats were moving slowly up and down the river, and I could hear the sound of an accordion soaring above a boisterous wind. I remember feeling that rapturous freedom and energy that only comes to the very young.

'The women of the world are beginning to affirm their independence in concrete ways'—this was what de Beauvoir had written in her introduction to *The Second Sex*. The leaves of her book rustled as I thought of my mother and the independence she affirmed. It had come at a price—separation from my father until the war came and went—but any other way would have been a life lived in falsehood. I thought of the pressures that still confined women's lives to traditional ways of existing, and it seemed to me that my own liberation as an adult began with de Beauvoir, whose words freed me from the dangerous world of 'untils'.

'Untils' tried to make young women believe that work was a fill-in until marriage, when some hapless male was supposed to bring home the bacon in return for obedience and dependency 'until death us do part'. 'Untils' aimed to indenture us to the male ego. 'Untils' reminded us of our place in the world.

In various classes at Sheffield High School, we had learned how to starch and turn men's shirt collars, read books in which the lives of women were invisible, and survive school uniform inspections to make sure that our tunics concealed our knickers and that we were not wearing patent leather shoes that might reflect our nether regions. I was about sixteen years old at the time, and thought these practices a joke.

It took many years before women began to reach any kind of equality with men. Looking back, it was as if a miasma of ignorance and neglect fogged the minds of humankind—and that's the generous interpretation. The other is a male desire for power. A memorable story concerns the feisty and clever Baroness Seear, leader of the Liberal Party in the House of Lords from 1984 to 1988, when she was trying to gain acceptance of sex discrimination legislation in the boardrooms of Britain. After a particularly vigorous argument, the chairman of one meeting leaned forward, tapped her kindly on the arm, and said, 'My dear lady, you mustn't think that we dislike women. We love 'em. Why, we have them at home.'

WOMEN THEN AND NOW

It does not appear that all men love women, even if they have them at home. Lying in bed recently, about ten o'clock at night, I listened to two helicopters flying overhead, sounding as if they might drop on my rooftop. A dark sullen sky was pierced by dazzling lights, diving, swooping, noises getting louder, as I resisted a glancing thought that this might be some kind of terrorist attack. Eventually I went to sleep. The following morning I heard that the helicopters were searching for two young men who were later charged with dragging a fourteen-year-old girl onto the beach near where I live, and raping her. What century are we living in, and how much longer do women have to endure the violence and humiliation of rape—in peace and in war?

From the internet and from my own photo library I find thumbnail pictures of decades of women struggling to obtain universal suffrage, or the right to vote. Women with flags and banners, women laughing and crying, women shouting through megaphones. Dates and numbers make dull reading, but not if you imagine the bravery of these women: women who chained themselves to public buildings, smashed windows, risked the wrath of their husbands, served terms in prison, went on hunger strikes.

Fighting for equality and justice did not end with the right to vote. It invaded and strengthened our everyday lives, particularly when the United Nations proclaimed the Universal Declaration of Human Rights that granted individuals—regardless of race, creed, gender, age or any other status—rights that they could use to challenge unjust law or oppressive customary practice. From that declaration of human rights, a whole raft of other human rights initiatives came into law. The genteel middle-class ladies of my mother's era who had clamoured for reform would never have guessed that by the sixties and seventies un-genteel middle-class ladies would be demanding revolution. Genteel women of old were anxious to point out that they did not seek to disrupt society or to unseat God. Women of the sixties and seventies did seek to disrupt society, and left God to His or Her own devices.

Am I right to use words like 'revolution' and 'battle'? I believe so. When I think about all women endured and continue to endure in efforts to attain justice, I don't believe this would have happened without battles, without revolution, and without risk. The battles continue, particularly in countries like Afghanistan, where women and girls, striving for education and for equality, can be punished by death or disfigurement. And where rape is a common occurrence, and women may well be jailed instead of the perpetrator.

1970s

FEMINISM

By the time Joshua was four, Ellis and I decided we wanted more time with our children, so we decided to take them to Italy for a year in 1972. When we returned to Australia it felt as though we were stepping into another world. Women were tangibly pushing for social and political change, as if this were the beginning of further change. Germaine Greer had only recently published *The Female Eunuch*, a book that was stirring our friends to fierce arguments.

'But do you hate men?' asked Ellis in an interview with Greer, and was swallowed up in her scorn.

'Ouch, that's a bit below the belt,' he replied.

'If you think I'm the slightest bit interested in what's below your belt, Mr Blain, you're very much mistaken.'

—

While Ellis and I had been away, many of my women friends had cropped their hair, donned baggy overalls or boiler suits, and started calling each other 'sister'. This was serious stuff—it didn't mean looking like a man, it meant getting down to business, PDQ.

I had barely arrived back in Sydney when I was asked to chair a Sydney University/ABC television series about 'the changing role of women'. I sat on a straight-backed chair, hands crossed in my lap, and said smugly, 'I'm very lucky—my husband doesn't mind if I work.' Too late, I realised what I'd said. It wasn't even what I thought, but what alarmed me was the ease with which I'd tossed out the phrase: *my husband doesn't mind if I work.*

'You need to be deconditioned, sister,' said a friend. I was happy to be deconditioned, but I wasn't sure I wanted to be everyone's sister. It didn't take me long to realise that in this new-found fight for equality, women needed sisters; we needed each other.

I discovered this immediately I became CEO of the Australian Film, Television and Radio School in 1985. AFTRS had never had a female director, and not one of its management staff was a woman. It was fairly obvious from the start that although the students were interested in discussing new ideas, some of the senior staff were far from happy. They muttered things like 'This is no job for a woman', asked me persistently if I were feeling tired, and drew my attention to graffiti drawn in the male toilets—which I went and inspected at the end of my second day. The first piece of graffiti depicted the former director, who was a gentle man and a brilliant teacher, blindfolded, hands tied together, and with a dagger sticking out of his back. In a separate charcoal drawing, I stood to the right of him, a noose around my neck, a trapdoor beneath my feet.

In the 1970s, life was tough if you were a woman and wanted interesting, well-paid work.

Australia, 1972

'IT'S TIME'

The seventies was a time of almost seismic change which wasn't immediately visible but made itself felt through a raft of human rights and equal opportunity legislation, and through women obtaining positions of authority or breaking out in surges of creative endeavours.

Change swept across the country like a tidal wave. IT'S TIME, said political posters and banners. On 2 December 1972, the Australian Labor Party won government after twenty-three years in opposition. On 8 December 1972, Gough Whitlam was appointed prime minister, and what were subsequently known as the Whitlam years came into being.

The new government pumped thought, energy and creativity into concerns that had long been neglected by Australian governments, including many areas that affected women: equal pay and equal employment opportunity; programs to ensure that girls had the same educational opportunities as boys; free university education; childcare funding; sales tax on contraceptive pill removed; oral contraceptives brought under the Pharmaceutical Benefits Scheme; and abortion laws eased in Victoria, New South Wales and South Australia. These were all on the agenda.

Attempts to establish a Royal Commission into abortion were debated throughout December 1973. In April 1974 the government announced there would be a Royal Commission on male and female relationships; the issue was shelved pending the election of that year and revived in August 1974 with the eventual title Royal Commission on Human Relationships.

For me and for so many women across Australia, the Whitlam government opened doors and windows to outside worlds, and allowed us to think change was possible, that discrimination against women would no longer be allowed. Consider just one infuriating instance that was overturned: *A separated woman with a good salary was denied a loan as a matter of policy.*

HUMAN RELATIONS

One evening in early spring of 1974, I was barbecuing sausages for the children when the phone rang and a lugubrious voice said, 'Dear lady, I am ringing to see if you would do a small job for the government.'

'What sort of job?' I said cautiously.

A cough. Silence. Followed by the words, 'My dear lady, I can't tell you yet, it's confidential.'

'Then how can I answer? I might say yes to digging up drains.'

'Haw haw,' said the voice. 'Certainly nothing like that.'

'Then may I guess?'

'Good idea. There's nothing that says you can't guess.'

So while Jonathan rescued the burning sausages, I began that old childhood guessing game, to which my mysterious caller responded with increasing excitement: 'Closer, closer; oh no, cold, very cold; now hot, getting hotter. BULLSEYE, dear lady! Bullseye!'

'Yes,' I said primly. 'Yes, I'd be very interested in the government's proposal.'

And that quaint story is how I eventually came to be a commissioner on the Royal Commission on Human

Relationships. The chair of the commission was a distinguished judge, Justice Elizabeth Evatt, and the other commissioner was the courageous and scholarly Most Reverend Felix Arnott, Anglican Archbishop of Brisbane. Our task: *To inquire into the family, social, educational, legal and sexual aspects of male–female relationships, with particular emphasis on responsible parenthood.* Which didn't leave much out.

Winston Churchill once said that Royal Commissions were like the ink in cuttlefish; they served to conceal rather than reveal. Many government members were concerned that the terms were so wide that the commission would be working forever to cover them. One correspondent to the newspapers felt that all such commissions were doomed to obscurity and neglect—'Remember the Vernon Commission? I thought you wouldn't.' Women's liberation groups argued that action was needed, not talk. Others didn't take it as seriously. In certain Canberra circles, because of the subject matter it came to be known as the 'Fucking Commission'. And on occasions when I'd encounter him at public meetings around Australia, the prime minister would cheerfully boom: 'Ah, and how is my sex commissioner?'

Various newspapers referred to the Report of the Royal Commission on Human Relationships as a 'worthless circus', 'a synonym for futility, procrastination and extravagance', 'a giant talk-back radio show', and 'an attempt to pry into the bedrooms of the nation'.

Later, after we'd handed in our five-volume report, the press were kinder. The *Age* said it was 'an extraordinary achievement for any government commission of inquiry'. *Pol* magazine described it as 'the most exhaustive study ever undertaken of the social customs of Australians'. David McNicoll of the *Bulletin* wrote of the hearings: 'I went to scoff and remained to pray.'

Our evidence was rich with accounts given by brave women and men of the persecution they received for being 'different'. Many people who were homosexual told us about lives of fear and persecution, of being ridiculed, robbed, beaten and blackmailed.

The situation and conditions of children with handicaps were also bleak: 'Some night staff change beds at midnight but the boys are not toileted and they can and do lie in urine and faeces all night. The stench is indescribable . . . these children are not animals, they are human beings.'

Women living in violent relationships had little protection: 'These women are being treated for anxiety and often reactions to their husband—thus one could say they are being treated for their husband's behaviour, for his "illness", rather than their understandable fear.'

It was no coincidence that similar inquiries had been instituted by countries all over the world. Recent years had seen technological and social change occur at an unparalleled pace—change that brought new stresses and new challenges to human relationships. Changes that I now reflect must have multiplied dramatically in the thirty or so years since that last commission of 1974: think of all the global and domestic challenges of the internet; think of warfare with its horrendous new killing machines; think of nuclear waste; of standards in education; of environmental hazards that threaten global deterioration, if not destruction. And alongside those cautionary tales consider overpopulation and starvation in so many countries around the world, while, in Australia, refugees who arrive in leaky boats are called illegals (which they are not) and are treated like pariahs instead of people who have lost everything and whose lives are often threatened unless they escape.

In order to collect our evidence, the commission departed from the formal and sometimes intimidating processes by which most Royal Commissions had previously operated. We visited capital cities and country towns. We travelled thousands of miles, from Bunbury in Western Australia to the Northern Territory 'milk run', a flight through remote inland settlements. We went to schools, shopping centres, sports fields, Aboriginal settlements, sheltered workshops, factories, refuges, rape crisis centres, abortion clinics, hospitals. We took evidence at public hearings, in private discussions, on the telephone, in writing, and in any other way the public wished to respond. Altogether we received thousands of informal submissions and over 1200 formal submissions in writing. Some were long research documents, many were handwritten letters, others were in the form of verse, drawings, audio tape and film. We mounted research projects on issues ranging from childcare to unreported rape. By the time we had finished, we had assembled a rich mosaic of the way people in Australia thought, felt and lived.

Our work was seriously threatened after the Whitlam government was denied supply during 1975, and we virtually had to close offices in 1976. During the early months of 1977, we three commissioners were writing the report. I remember being at home, in the summer heat, writing page after page as we tried to bring our work to completion. On 22 November 1977, we presented the final report of the Royal Commission on Human Relationships to the governor-general, John Kerr, right in the middle of a tumultuous election campaign. Whitlam had recently proclaimed from the steps of Parliament House: 'God save the Queen, because nothing will save the governor-general.'

The governor-general received us at Government House in Canberra; as he wobbled towards me he appeared to have drunk rather too much. 'Tell me, my dear,' he said. 'My wife and I sat up in bed nearly all night reading that bit of your report about lesbians. Tell me, we couldn't imagine how they do it. How *do* they do it?'

'Use your imagination, sir,' was my reply.

One week before its scheduled public release, the report was leaked to the press. What followed was like a Victorian melodrama. Anything controversial was taken out of context and sensationalised.

The prime minister, Malcolm Fraser, blamed Opposition Leader Gough Whitlam for the report, saying that it was appalling and that parts of it would fill every family in Australia with horror. He then admitted that he hadn't read it. Other government members nonetheless concurred with his assessment.

Whitlam then accused the government of resorting to the politics of smut, and said, 'You get the prefect and the fag getting a report, and looking under the desk for all the dirty bits.'

Quotes from members of the public varied from rapturous praise to wild indignation. 'It is a sick and misguided government, and every parent in Australia and every decent man and woman will oppose its introduction,' wrote Reuben F. Scarf from the Festival of Light. 'The Blessed Virgin be praised for the findings of the Royal Commission on Human Relationships,' wrote Maireadh Flannagan, mother of ten, from O'Malley in the Australian Capital Territory.

Because the release of the report had been delayed until after the election campaign—no reason was ever given—and then given to selected members of the right-wing press, I decided to release it immediately to remaining members of the press. So I went out at night, with copies of the report piled high in my boot. From time to time, I would look over my shoulder to make sure I wasn't being followed.

14

Into Africa

Between 1975 and 1995, I helped make some twenty-five documentary films in different parts of Africa and South-East Asia. Most of them were about deliverance—not in a biblical sense, but about countries struggling to find justice as they emerged from centuries of colonisation. They were about families suffering from famine and disease; about adults and children queuing in the hot sun, hoping to have one hour's free education; about women risking rape as they walked along dried-up riverbeds in search of water. They were about dire need. They were also about recovery.

Ethiopia, 1975

THE END OF EVERYTHING

When I first saw starvation, I cried. The year was 1975 and I was in Ethiopia, on the fringes of the Ogaden Desert following civil war and three years of famine in the country. Burning sand, fierce sun, corpses wrapped in hessian bags waiting to be buried—vertically, so the hyenas couldn't dig them up—bleached-white bones of camels and goats; old men who could scarcely walk, hobbling towards me, bony arms outstretched, pleading for food. Babies with swollen bellies and stick-thin legs, wailing.

I tried to hide my tears. Don, our cameraman, put an arm around my shoulders. 'It's okay. We all do it. Here, take this.' And he pushed a tissue into my hand.

The Ethiopian film was my introduction to an extraordinary cast of people who seemed to circle the globe in endless permutations, many of them addicted to providing aid. Over time I met priests, arms dealers, doctors and nurses; executive directors of companies selling heavy vehicles to Africa and then setting up factories to service them; bureaucrats of various political hues; mercenaries, journalists, UN officials and pilots. It was a long and varied list.

I admired the selflessness and courage of aid workers, who often found themselves in difficult and dangerous situations. Sometimes, though, I became puzzled over the ability of aid organisations to make the most bizarre mistakes, like the large consignment of American aid sent to help the flood victims of Bangladesh which turned out to be electric blankets, king size and queen. Or the German aid organisation which arrived in Somalia with surgical teams equipped to perform open-heart surgery when the most urgent need was for saline drips.

International aid has become one of the biggest businesses in the world. People are employed at all levels, from top diplomats and bureaucrats, chief executives of giant non-government aid agencies, health professionals, agronomists and economists to raw recruits from the cities who move from one aid camp to another, picking up jobs as they go.

Underpinning these dramas are serious political issues. How much value is western aid to third world countries if their interest debts by now exceed their loans? Who benefits from such exchanges? Have we substituted imperial colonialism for colonialism of the economic kind? These are the sorts of issues that are frequently discussed—often at the end of the day.

—

Addis Ababa, the capital of Ethiopia, looked as if a heap of rusty iron had been dropped from a great height. Dilapidated shacks, open drains, meagre shops and markets, a few blocks of workers' apartments. A hilly ramshackle town and, in the centre, the only hotel where foreigners were then allowed to stay, a splendid edifice in shining white marble that, inside, looked like a stage set for the opera *Aida*.

We spent a lot of time in that hotel, waiting in the foyer for government officials who never arrived, for travel permits to go to the Ogaden Desert that never came, for meetings with government ministers who had already left town, and for Solomon Lulu, our official guide.

Disaster experts paraded before us in a saraband of deals and counter-deals, gossip and innuendo . . . The Russians are searching for oil . . . Ethiopia will win the war in the Ogaden because Cuban troops will soon arrive to help us . . . Ethiopia will lose the war because America is giving tanks and planes to Somalia . . . The nomads are being asked to leave their nomadic life and become farmers—it won't work . . . The hotel is offering a Bavarian dinner with special Bavarian sausages and Bavarian potato pancakes . . . The German Ambassador won't attend because he is having an affair with the wife of the Ethiopian Minister for Social Stability.

A squad of earnest-looking men suddenly hustled by, on their way to a tour billed as 'A Flight to Hell and Back Again'. They were bound for the Ogaden Desert and their first taste of famine. They wore short-sleeved safari suits and clutched cardboard lunchboxes. The film director and I had a bet about whether the boxes contained Diet Coke.

—

On the road to the desert to begin our filming, the colours kept changing, from sweeps of saffron and orange to a startling blood red. The sand was dotted with gleaming white bones, flesh picked clean, skulls and legs and rib cages. Vultures hovered. One of the camera crew tugged at my arm as our jeep bounded over the sand dune. He pointed to a speck on the horizon which slowly grew into an ominous black stain and then into the strangest of sights, a huge gathering of people marooned in an ocean of sand.

Our driver brought his jeep to a halt and rubbed his eyes. 'Nomads. Arab invaders called them Turags. It means "lost souls". But the Turags call themselves Imochagh, "the free ones".'

The free ones teetered towards us. Children whose bones protruded like pieces of jagged stone and whose heads were grotesquely large. Women clutching babies to wizened breasts. Men with bow legs. No one spoke. I remembered this from my last visit. It's called 'the silence of starvation'.

Two army trucks were parked neatly on the outskirts of the crowds, side by side as if they were in a big city square. Soldiers were ladling grain from sacks stamped A GIFT FROM THE PEOPLE OF AUSTRALIA. Which people? I wondered. Children scrabbled under the truck for spills while a naked baby thrust a handful of dirt into her mouth.

The trucks had driven a thousand kilometres from the seaport of Djibouti and would only come once a month. The corn would last a family three days. Small children would not be able to digest the grain because it needed to be ground. There was no mill.

While we waited, a large group of people had gathered around a well into which a young man was being lowered by ropes so that he could fill buckets of water by hand. Behind the people, camels were also waiting patiently, their feet hobbled, their bones like umbrella spokes, their humps collapsed into withered bags of skin. Question: How did the camel lose its hump? Answer: It consumed it. But now that the hump was gone, the camel would die.

The camels were waiting for their names to be called to drink the water. Some camels waited for three days. 'The Turags love their camels,' said our driver. 'They know their tracks and the tracks of others'; they can tell the tribes that own them, whether a camel is ridden or is free, where it has been grazing and when it was last watered.

'They have never seen their camels dying. It is not in their folklore. When the camels go, it is the end of everything,'

Uganda, 1979

REIGN OF TERROR

One Sunday morning after we have come back from the beach one of my grandchildren is leaning across the kitchen table, looking at an old photograph of me in the *Australian*, dated 16 May 1979. The caption underneath the photograph reads: UGANDANS FED TO CROCODILES.

'Is that true? Did they try and feed you to crocodiles?'

'No, the crocodiles said I was too old.'

'But what if they hadn't said too old? What if they'd wanted to eat you?'

'I'd have run away.'

'You don't run very fast.'

'Fast enough.'

'But why did they want to feed people to the crocodiles?'

'Because there was a horrible president called Idi Amin and that's what he did. He was cruel.'

'Did the crocodiles know he was cruel?'

'No, because all they wanted was their dinner. They didn't think that was cruel.'

'But what if they didn't like humans?'

'Oh, but I think they did.'

'Did this Idi man kill lots of people?'

'Lots.'

'How many lots?'

'Thousands of lots, but now let's change the subject.'

'Why?'

'Because it upsets me.'

The subject is changed. With difficulty. This is edge-of-darkness stuff and my grandchildren are at an age when they are beginning to enjoy the macabre.

—

Idi Amin Dada, later known as the 'Butcher of Uganda', was president of Uganda from 1971 to 1979. He had joined the British colonial army in 1946 as an assistant cook and rose steadily through the ranks. The British Foreign Office described him as 'a splendid type and a good football player'—the kind of remark that seemed apt for a British foreign officer in the fifties and sixties. The good football player rapidly showed he had other talents. Such as killing.

After seizing power in a military coup, Amin bestowed on himself a string of titles: His Excellency President for Life, Field Marshal Al Hadji Doctor Idi Amin Dada, VC, DSO, MC, Lord of the Beasts of the Earth and Fishes of the Sea and Conqueror of the British Empire in Africa in General and Uganda in Particular—in addition to his officially stated claim of being the uncrowned King of Scotland.

Up to half a million people were murdered during Amin's reign of terror. They were stabbed, hanged, hammered to death or fed to his crocodiles. His rule was characterised by every conceivable human rights abuse, and scarcely a person living in Uganda escaped the attention of his secret police.

Amin's rule came to an end when he attempted to annex a section of neighbouring Tanzania. A combined force of Tanzanians and former Ugandan citizens drove Amin's army back into Uganda, and then withdrew. Amin's excesses, together with his failed military attacks, had left Uganda depleted and its people starving. Inflation in Uganda was running at 300 per cent a year. Amin was forced to flee.

In 1979, I paid my first visit to Uganda. I went with an international aid team to film the turmoil in the country and to document urgent aid requirements. When we arrived, Amin had just fled, leaving his troops to fight lone gun battles from hills surrounding Kampala, the capital. This was the shooting we heard every night, and we hoped it wouldn't come any nearer.

One of our first visits in Kampala was to the Ugandan State Research Bureau: an L-shaped pink building set among trees and gardens of pink roses. It looked like a prosperous downtown motel anywhere in the world, but this was Idi Amin's slaughterhouse, his secret police headquarters: a place of interrogation and torture, of imprisonment without trial, where people disappeared and were never seen again—and where, night after night, Amin would get drunk with a small group of soldiers and, for his amusement, watch as several hundred prisoners were killed, men in one line, women and children in another. Men were forced to murder each other with a sledgehammer. Club the man in front of you, then it will be your turn. Women were strangled with heavy wires. Children were shot. Why the differentiation? I wondered. Why not keep women in the clubbing line? Not nicely, surely? And then I realised: women might not have the strength to club anyone to death.

Prisoners were kept in rooms that were three metres by four metres. Sixty people per room. Men, women, children. No latrines. A bucket in the corner for urinating and defecating. Guards fed the prisoners as and when they liked. Once, prisoners went sixteen days without food and were forced to drink each other's urine. Those who were waiting to be executed could see corpses from last night's savagery piled outside the pink garden walls.

Three thousand secret police kept the State Research Bureau filled to overflowing. 'We are above the law,' said one man, patting the small dark identity card he carried in the breast pocket of his brightly coloured floral shirt. They all seemed to wear brightly coloured floral shirts. My man described his job of investigation and killing as if it were some kind of hobby. 'I am paid good money, yes, for every persons I report,' he said, lighting a cigarette and drawing on it with an air of self-importance.

Amin and his soldiers had left in a hurry when the Tanzanian troops moved in. Upstairs, filing cabinets were upturned, papers strewn across the floor: passports, identity cards, notebooks. Other rooms were full of boxes of ammunition, grenades, machine guns. Downstairs, in the torture chambers, we found a different kind of horror: family snapshots, toys, a human scalp topped by a mop of black hair, a prayer book. The smell of fear, the smell of death. Walls and floors caked with dried blood, odd bits of clothing swimming in wet blood, a red thong, a black shoe, a woman's green floral dress, the faeces of terrified victims. A terrible smell of putrefaction hung over everything and everyone, including us.

We filmed some of the rooms and the underground dungeons, and I took a few items home with me in case we needed more evidence. I put everything in two cardboard boxes which I later stored in my garden shed. When I began writing, I went to my shed and found the boxes, opened them, and felt sick.

A faded green file was marked: A PLOT TO KILL HE IDI DADA AMIN. Inside was a typed letter:

Dear Idi, I am a great supporter of your kill anti-white policies. Therefore, I feel that it is my responsibility to inform you about a CIA plot to kill you. I am an employee of U.S. consulte, 5 days back just by chance I learned about such plot. They have planned to send two professional murderers from Tehrans some time early 76. Therefore, you must ban every Iranian entry to Uganda. Signed: A Sympathiser.

I pulled out two T-shirts. White. Block-printed on the front in large black lettering: IDI AMIN DADA, KING OF AFRICA, CONQUEROR OF THE BRITISH EMPIRE, CARRIED BY THE BRITISH IN UGANDA. Behind the lettering was a picture of Amin being carried by two blurry figures. Amin is black. The figures are white. They hold Amin aloft on a sedan chair. Their heads are bowed. Why did they carry him—because otherwise they would have been killed? I can only guess this was the reason. But who were they, and where are they now?

Slowly, I emptied the boxes. I almost expected a genie of evil to fly away, until I realised there was no genie; there was only a mad and wicked man.

More papers fell out of an old cloth bag—a blue card and a scrap of dirty paper, once the property of Nsubuga Joshua Luzinda, electrical engineer, date of issue 2 December 1977. The photograph shows a young boy in a crisply ironed floral shirt; he smiles. Is he Luzinda's son?

Another document, dog-eared, shiny black cover, name blotted out in purple, older man, white shirt, tie, age thirty-five. At the back is a photograph of a little boy, aged about two, wearing pink floral overalls and clutching a teddy bear. He is sitting in a field of grass and laughing. A half-page for a wife's signature is blurred.

I leaned back in my garden chair and let a summer's breeze calm me as I remembered the words of a young priest we met when we were first exploring the dungeons. He was a big man who had been shrunk by his experiences. His name was Joseph—Joseph of the high forehead and wide smile that kept disappearing and reappearing as if he wasn't quite sure where he was. He had been held captive for three months, every night shuffling along in the line, and every night refusing to hammer the man in front.

'Why they did not kill me, I do not know. Perhaps my robes,' he said, his voice reverberating in the dungeons. He would be pulled away, alcohol thrown in his face, kicked, bashed and dragged back to his cell. For three months this torture continued. His initial crime? Unknowingly, he had parked alongside Idi Amin's car and he was arrested as a dangerous citizen. A spy. To this day he does not know what happened to his wife and three children.

We were leaving the dungeons with Joseph when he stopped and looked around him. He shook his head in disbelief. 'Vanity, vanity, all is vanity.' He said this very quietly, tears running down his cheeks.

—

In the taxi going back to our hotel the driver stopped so we could buy fruit—melons, oranges and lemons, pomegranates. We sat by the side of the road to have orange juice and a bottle of water. The taxi driver joined us. He was a modest-looking man with a gentle manner and he spoke good English. I asked him how the country could possibly have recovered after so many years of Amin's insanity. He looked at me, then said quietly, 'We had so much sorrow we had to make up. What else could we do? Go on killing? I don't think so.'

Uganda, 1994

'It's all right to take your handbag into the street, ma'am,' says the concierge at the Kampala hotel, smiling as he waves his hand. The first time I went to Uganda it was not all right to walk the streets, carrying money or anything else. There were enough tales of people having arms severed by swooping motorbike duos—one person drove, the other hacked. 'Now it is safe,' beams the man at the hotel.

Rwanda, 1994

A TALE OF HORROR

In 1994, I went to Rwanda during the genocide, when nearly one million people, mostly Tutsis, were burned or hacked to death during the space of six weeks. The dead of Rwanda accumulated at nearly three times the rate of Jewish dead during the Holocaust. It was the most efficient mass killing since the atomic bombings of Hiroshima and Nagasaki, even though the most primitive instruments of death were used: machetes. Good serviceable implements, made for farming, not for hacking off heads and limbs.

Just two of us had gone—me and a cameraman—to gather news footage for the ABC. I went because it seemed important to be there, to bear witness, but as we drew nearer I was beginning to have doubts about my capacity to cope.

The rain was heavy as we approached the border and I could barely make out the wooden sign: BIENVENUE A LA REPUBLIQUE DE RWANDA. Mounds of bodies lay by the side of the road, haphazardly thrown into piles, arms and legs sticking out at awkward angles, the sour smell of death as we wound down the windows to clear the mist, soldiers with guns, and an air of seedy desolation common to frontier posts around the world.

Buildings, sheds and outhouses had barred windows and were lit up by searchlights so that I could see soldiers with rifles, cigarette butts at their feet, and hear a cacophony of music from several large radios. Armed guards wearing blue UN berets motioned us to stop. More UN soldiers were gathered on the verandah of a large wooden shed, drinking Coca-Cola. A polyglot of nationalities: Canadians, Algerians, Somalis, a couple of British soldiers, and a young woman in black jeans from the French humanitarian agency Médecins Sans Frontières. Further up the road, in a second shed, a captain from Botswana and a major from Pakistan warmed themselves in front of a brazier. The major wore a blue silk scarf knotted around his neck. He asked me if I had seen the new play by Pinter which had recently opened in London.

'No,' I said apologetically. 'No, I haven't.' I looked around and wondered what these men were doing here, this major from Pakistan and the captain from Botswana. The soldiers from Canada, Tunisia and the Sudan. The French aid worker, in her tight black T-shirt and black jeans. Why were any of them here, playing music, smoking cigarettes, risking their lives in a war not of their making? Probably many of them had not even heard of Rwanda until they were sent. They had no authority to stop the killings and there were too few of them, but nevertheless they were here because since the founding of the UN, nations have haltingly undertaken a global responsibility for keeping peace in the world. American political satirist P.J. O'Rourke called it 'playing Nanny'.

The rain was now drumming on the iron roof like bullets. The major asked us if we would sign the security records, a large school exercise book with a red cover on which was printed GOD IS LOVE. I asked him if he'd been able to stand by and do nothing as men, women and children had been hacked to death or burned alive. The major said that people expected too much of the UN. It could only do those things its member nations permitted and supported.

Once over the border and clear of the UN compounds, we drove along a road that was blackened on either side. The stumps of farm buildings looked like blackened teeth protruding from faces of devastation. Buzzards beat their wings over muddy ponds. Steady trickles of refugees carrying food and bedding on their heads shuffled along the road, going to Kigali, the capital. Our driver told us that people paid money to their killers, begging them to use bullets instead of knives.

A very old man squatted by the side of the road trying to sell a scraggy goat. Three girls in bright yellow waved at our jeep.

We were looking to interview an emergency medical team and found one on the outskirts of Kigali, in a large iron shed that had been turned into a makeshift hospital. It was hot and dark. At one end, lit by spotlights, a small bundle lay on a trestle bed. I approached and found a frightened child, moaning softly. He had trodden on a landmine and was about to have his leg amputated—even though there was no running water, inadequate anaesthetics and poor lighting. A Swedish nurse administered the anaesthetic and stroked the child's forehead. The surgeon, a handsome greying Italian, urged on a young Australian army captain who was performing the operation. She had earlier described herself to me as 'a mother of two from Maroubra'. This was the first time she had cut off anyone's leg, let alone a child's. She was scared.

'Harder, harder,' said the Italian war surgeon, his theatre cap ballooning sideways at a drunken angle. 'You are not cutting a chicken bone.'

When the operation was over I talked to the surgeon, who was now pacing up and down outside the shed, a cigarette dangling from his mouth. This was a man who had spent the last twenty years moving from one war zone to the next and, in between, lobbying at the United Nations in New York to see an end to landmines. Again, I wondered about his role in this African tragedy. And the young woman from Maroubra, and the Swedish nurse. Why were they here? The boy was still unconscious, his body writhing like an eel that had been chopped in two. I stroked his forehead and felt helpless.

—

From Rwanda, we travelled across the border to Zaire, where nearly a million refugees were huddled on a square mile of black volcanic rock. Many of them were Hutus who had participated in the slaughter of Tutsis and, later, fled from their crimes. As I've described, some were boys as young as eight who carried Kalashnikovs and swaggered in front of us to show off their newfound power. Ahead, wagons from all the aid agencies in the world crisscrossed the treeless ground, their pennants flying like crusader flags in the acrid air. Only they weren't waging war, they were waging peace. The French were in charge of water supplies, the British were building shelters, the Canadians brought in ambulances, the Australians provided medical teams. Belgian drivers rode huge earth-moving tractors that looked like creatures from some prehistoric age heaving themselves over the barren rock.

A young man who was standing in front of a UN truck said that the UN had asked for eighty water tanks from foreign donors. Only twelve arrived. 'It's sexier to feed people than help them shit in a safe place,' he said in despair.

Despair also came from a French army captain as he stamped out a cigarette with his boot. 'We've lost the body count. We're a transport regiment, not morticians.'

But as his soldiers chucked bodies into waiting trucks, he gently admonished them, 'Softly, be compassionate, these are human beings—they could have been your mother or your father.' When I heard those words I wanted to cry.

In a children's camp I talked to doctors, nurses and psychologists who had come from around the world to help children who were deeply traumatised. A child of about ten was sitting on the ground, rocking back and forth. He put his fingers in his ears as his mouth opened and closed in silent screams.

'He has seen his mother and father killed,' said an aid worker. 'Horror has taken away his voice.'

'My oh my,' said a woman's voice behind me. 'Look at that cute little fellow with those great big eyes. I just want to take him home and love him.'

—

That night, back at the aid camp in Kigali where we were billeted, I gazed at shadows flickering against the canvas tent. The effect became hypnotic as I found myself thinking back over wars in my lifetime. Wars driven by fear or revenge. Grandiose and greedy wars. Wars where the euphemism 'ethnic cleansing' brought shudders to the world. Wars that led to compromised peace processes and the seeds of future wars. A grotesque daisy chain of wars: *They kill me, they kill me not, they kill me, they kill me not. They kill.*

I fell asleep, only to wake quite late to hear a woman's voice call out, 'Cooee . . . Cooee. I say, I say, is anybody there?'

I dragged myself out of my sleeping bag, grabbed a sarong and a T-shirt, and went outside to see a large woman with a bright floral sarong wrapped around her ample middle. On top she wore a purple tunic, and her shoes were sensible brogues. She gave me a handshake that made me wince.

'Sister Helen, Anglican nun from Kenya,' she boomed in an English accent. 'Came when I heard that thirty of our order were bumped off in the first wave of killings.'

'Did you find any alive?'

'I most certainly did. Four of 'em, all Tutsi youngsters, hiding in the rafters of a neighbouring Tutsi house. Could have lost their own lives.'

I reflected that the anomaly of this terrible genocide was that Hutus and Tutsis had lived together in peace for decades. They had intermarried, worked together, played together. Sister Helen said she aimed to bring nuns from all over the world to Kigali, to pray and work for healing and for peace. She invited us to the Feast of the Assumption.

'Tomorrow evening, seven o'clock, Archbishop's residence. Women only. But be jolly careful walking through the garden. Landmines.'

—

On the way to the Archbishop's residence, trees loomed in strange tasselled shapes, frogs croaked in the bushes, and the only illumination came from a yellow rind of moon lying spent on its back. The building had been badly shelled and burned. Broken doors and windows were barricaded with heavy pieces of wood. Darkness grew into light as we turned the corner and were confronted by an enormous, lavishly painted banqueting hall lit by myriad tiny candles that threw pinpoints of white on the walls and ceilings. The hall was filled with nuns. Nuns of all nationalities and ages. Nuns in robes of every colour—scarlet, pink, green, blue, purple, and the customary brown and black. A nattering of nuns.

Sister Helen welcomed us. 'Women were never allowed here. Men only. The Archbishop and his chaps. Probably turning in his grave. Whoops. He hasn't got a grave and serve him jolly well right. He was a baddy. Went with the other side. Got himself shot. Good riddance and may God save his soul.'

'A hard task,' observed the dry voice of an older nun, robed in brown.

A long table in the middle of the hall bore the feast, made by the nuns from scraps of food: platters of crackers, each topped with a small sliver of tomato plus a bowl of rice, some bananas, a few small bottles of brightly coloured fizzy drink, three jugs of water. In the centre of the table, surrounded by candles and flowers, was a glass bowl full of bright yellow custard, lovingly decorated with crumbled biscuits and slices of banana which carefully spelled the words *Bonne fête*.

'Sister Helen found the custard powder. She's very clever,' whispered one of the younger nuns.

At this point, Sister Helen dived under the table and from between her legs triumphantly produced several large unlabelled bottles. She uncorked the first and poured out six glasses of ruby-red wine. 'Don't ask where that came from,' she roared, as the nuns giggled and fluttered, their voices floating upwards to the gilded rafters of the banqueting hall. 'It won't turn into blood, but that's all right because we don't have any bread.'

INTERVENTION

The story of Rwanda became a tale of horror when the UN was unable to get American support for intervention. Bill Clinton, who was then the US president, remembered the failure of President George Bush senior in Somalia in 1992, when he promised that 3000 marines would be 'in by Christmas and out by the new year'. Six years later the marines were still in Somalia.

America used the pretext that what was happening in Rwanda was not a genocide and so it was not bound by UN regulations. The argument was sustained for weeks as world leaders wrestled with the problem of how many people had to die before a genocide could be proclaimed. While the US State Department was engaged in this delicate debate with itself, Hutu extremists had already killed almost a million people in their bid to wipe out every Tutsi in the country. Intelligence reports showed that the Rwandan cabinet and almost certainly the president knew of a planned 'final solution to eliminate all Tutsis' before the slaughter reached its peak.

When help did arrive it was too little, too late. The killings were largely over. Corpses swollen in the river, corpses burned in the churches. The west initially tried to pass it off as civil war, then as a tribal war. It was neither. It was genocide.

The Canadian army colonel in charge of peacekeeping in Rwanda had cabled the UN urging immediate intervention. His request was ignored. When the killings began he cabled again saying that 1500 soldiers would be sufficient to quell the rampage. One thousand of his troops were withdrawn and he was left with fifty. Fifty young men with orders not to take up arms but to do the best they could. Belgium peacekeepers, ordered to withdraw, threw their epaulettes on the ground in disgust.

As we, in Australia, watched from our living rooms the butchering of men, women and children, there was little global pressure for the UN to respond. Perhaps too many people saw this as yet another African problem. Would this have been allowed to happen had the slaughtered Tutsis been white? Almost certainly the answer would be no.

This shameful lack of international response to the horror in Rwanda led me to start exploring the nature and significance of international intervention. The challenge of peace is to decide at what point international military intervention is justified and under what grounds. Who makes the decisions and whose soldiers should participate, third world or first? Is there a role for mercenaries, and under whose control?

'Deliverance from Evil' was the title of Kofi Annan's address on 20 September 1999 to the last UN General Assembly session of the twentieth century. Humanitarian intervention in the twenty-first century was his subject. In his soft voice he pointed out that the notion of state sovereignty, central to the concept of the UN, is being redefined by the forces of globalisation and international cooperation. 'We have to think anew about how the world responds to humanitarian crises,' he said.

Rwanda showed the importance of early intervention, the need to understand the danger of conflict early, to prevent developments reaching the point where violence was inevitable, and to recognise how far into the past grudges might reach. Often there was need for fundamental reconciliation, and this could only be achieved by a willingness and ability to listen to all the dramatically different stories told by people who were involved in the conflict. Tales from the Persian Gulf, Kosovo, Timor, Cyprus and Northern Ireland have all shown that if people can feel their common humanity, miracles sometimes happen.

Mozambique, February 1991

LANDING ON A MINE

Every time I made a film in Africa there was always the chance of something untoward happening. Untoward is an old-fashioned word that mitigates against nastiness. Untoward is dignified, polite, contained. Unexpectedly landing on a bomb is not dignified or contained. 'Not very sensible, old girl,' my father said when he heard the news. Yet our plane did land on a mine and we survived.

We were making a film about famine and terrorism in the fledgling democracy of Mozambique. Famine was caused by drought and by the brutalising of the country by Renamo, a terrorist movement largely funded by powerful white business interests in South Africa, Portugal, the United States and former Rhodesia. Its orders were to destroy Mozambique's fragile independence by fierce attacks on civilians, particularly in rural areas in the north. Over 200,000 innocent men, women and children had already been killed, tortured, or driven from their homes. Refugees were hiding in border camps, mostly in neighbouring Malawi, too frightened to return.

Our first brief sent us flying to an area where Renamo had recently torched several villages, and mutilated or killed with random cruelty. As we circled to land I gazed down at paddocks of parched grey stubble, a few thatched huts, and a small gathering of people. Just as we touched ground there was a loud explosion and we were violently thrown from one side of our seats to the other. After the plane had shuddered to a halt, everyone raced for the exit door, frightened of fire. I stayed. I thought we had struck a rock. Then I heard someone shouting, 'Move it, Anne, the whole bloody plane might explode.' I moved it.

Outside, we walked gingerly around the plane, trying not to trip over the tussocks of grass. It was easy to see what had happened. We had landed on a mine that had blown off a wheel and blasted a hole in the plane's undercarriage, perilously close to where we had been sitting. This was preferable to blasting a hole in us, but it wasn't a pleasant experience. Automatically, we pulled out our cameras. Then we froze. If there was one landmine, almost certainly there were more. 'After you,' we said to each other with exaggerated courtesy, no one wanting to take the first steps off the field.

There were four of us in the film crew, plus Charlie, an interpreter from the capital, Maputo. He was a mild-mannered young man who wore dark glasses and kept assuring us he cared for our safety. Our bullshit detector told us to believe him. The headman from the village, clad in jeans and a red T-shirt advertising Camel cigarettes, led us between a double line of villagers—men, women and children—who sang and danced and clapped their hands. They seemed to take the landmine incident as a common event. While we were being feted and given bottles of Coke, we noticed half a dozen elderly men from the village walking up and down the landing field, prodding it with long poles.

'Mine detectors,' said the headman, whose name was Joe. He was thin and grizzled with tightly curled grey hair. When we asked why he didn't send his cattle to run across the field he grinned and said, 'Cattle too much money. More money than men.'

When the time came to leave, we were lent bicycles to reach the next destination. 'You must stay on the track. Do not go on the grass,' said Charlie. His voice was stern. 'Otherwise, bang bang and goodbye one leg—maybe two leg. Landmines LIKE hiding in grass. Like baby chickens. Chickens also LIKE hiding in grass.' He laughed uproariously.

'Plenty landmines in Mozambique,' said the headman, who had joined us. 'Plenty terrorist.' Now it was his turn to laugh uproariously. I laughed with faint enthusiasm. I was familiar with the danger of landmines, but I had never thought I would land on one. That was something that happened to other people, not to me.

I set off, determined to keep on course, riding a bike that skidded along the narrow track. Sun beat on the back of my neck, even though I kept pulling down my khaki hat. My four male companions were ahead of me. About twenty minutes later, they braked, put down their bikes and solemnly lined up side by side as if they were dressed in business suits and fronting a western-style urinal instead of a crumbling ditch. With precision timing, they sprayed a fountain into the air.

I could not follow their example for one simple reason: I had the wrong anatomy. The only way I could pee into the ditch was by jumping into it and risking setting off an explosive device. Or disturbing a Mozambique spitting cobra, capable of ejecting venom up to 2.4 metres. I'd only just learned about the spitting cobra and it sounded worse than a landmine. I cast aside modesty and squatted on the road.

—

Australian troops had learned about landmines first-hand in
the Vietnam War. I remembered that. And, with a little more
insight, I realised how much courage it must have taken to leave
their camps. Just before I left, when I was going through my
files, I found an old newspaper cutting of a soldier's account
of what it was like in Vietnam in 1969, when landmines were
a constant threat:

> Every time we stepped outside the wire, we who went
> first thought about mines a lot. Every second of every
> minute of every hour of every day of every week of every
> month . . . With every other aspect of combat you have a
> fighting chance: you can shoot back, you can take cover,
> you can run. With mines, they say the last thing you hear
> before you are maimed or killed is a single soft click. I'd
> ask my friends who stepped on them, Mick, Binky, Peter,
> but they never lived to tell me. What's left of those who did
> survive, usually can't remember. The funny thing they look
> like part of a child's toy. A plastic bit off a car engine. So
> inoffensive. Yet they are the most offensive of all the cruel
> weapons of war.

Already, on previous visits to Africa—to Ethiopia, the Sudan,
Somalia and Rwanda—I had encountered children with their
limbs blown off by landmines, men and women who had lost
the legs and arms and hands they needed to farm and to feed
their families . . . 'The most offensive of all the cruel weapons
of war,' the soldier had written. I believe he was right.

—

On the flight from Australia to Maputo, I'd pulled out my map of Mozambique to see quite clearly that two great rivers, the Zambezi and the Limpopo, divided the country. I said the word 'Limpopo', trying to recall an evasive memory from childhood. And then it came to me: 'The great grey-green, greasy Limpopo.' Of course, Rudyard Kipling's *Just So Stories*! I was six, and sitting on my father's knee, turning the pages while he read to me as I tried not to wriggle with excitement in case he told me to get down.

I took another look at the map and saw that where we were going wasn't far from the great grey-green greasy Limpopo River and, like a child, I felt unexpectedly excited. I also felt the passing of a shadow. The child could stay within the story, but the adult had to drop back into the reality of a deeply troubled country.

For some 400 years, Mozambique was colonised by the Portuguese, who exploited its mineral wealth, encouraged a brutal slave trade, and turned its capital city, Maputo, into a playground for the rich. But in 1975, after ten years of civil war, and a succession of freedom movements in other African territories, the people of Mozambique won their independence. Virtually overnight, the Portuguese withdrew. In anger, they burned buildings and farms, killed livestock, drove tractors over cliff tops, destroyed maps of sewer lines and, in a final burst of spite, poured concrete down toilets and washbasins. They left behind a country in ruins: no infrastructure, no educational or legal systems, a literacy rate of only 5 per cent, one-third of its children dying before the age of one.

You would never have guessed this from a casual look around Maputo, a city that was known in its early years as

Lourenço Marques, after Vasco da Gama's navigator, who first sailed into its broad and beautiful harbour in 1544. By the early nineteenth century it had become a prosperous Mediterranean-style city, containing handsome examples of colonial architecture. In 1991, some buildings were still in ruins from the Portuguese withdrawal, but most of the deliberate damage had been repaired.

—

We drove into Maputo through pouring rain, over potholes in the road, past palm trees waving in vigorous health. Our hearts lifted at the sight of handsome old colonial buildings, and sea-front cafes in bright blues, greens and pinks. It was so lovely it was almost impossible to believe this had been a war zone. Yet now, Maputo is a beautiful city, with wide boulevards, and a promenade that curves along the length of the shoreline. There the rich tourists were dining in their tropical linens, looking as if they had escaped from a John le Carré novel. The rain had stopped and the sun shone.

Most people seemed to be lunching outside at a cluster of blue and white seafood restaurants, where groups of musicians gathered round outdoor tables, playing music that made me want to dance. I smelled fresh fish, grilled on hot coals with garlic and lemon, tamarind and ginger. I wanted to eat.

'Later,' murmured the others.

'Later,' I agreed. Reluctantly.

We left the harbour front and walked down narrow streets beneath high green shuttered windows. Large earthenware pots stood on either side of doorways. White cotton curtains billowed out of open windows. Black and white rugs decorated hallways. Walls were hung with long plaits of fresh marigolds and hollyhocks—orange, pink and blue. We turned a corner and discovered a huge and joyful market, bursting with colour—red and green peppers, purple aubergines, melons and bananas, lobster tails, shrimp and prawns, and woven straw baskets in yellow, orange, pink and blue.

Round another corner, we met a bearded barber wearing sandals and a short white barber's coat, tied at the back. The walls of his shop were hung with old leather straps, while polished cutthroat razors lay on his tabletop, side by side. Outside, a child danced on the pavement. His child? I wondered.

We were staying in the city while we tried to get an interview with President Joaquim Chissano, Mozambique's second president. The country's first president, Samora Machel, and many members of his cabinet were killed on 19 October 1986, not long after Mozambique achieved independence, when their plane mysteriously crashed near the border with South Africa. Machel's widow, Graça, was convinced that the plane crash was not an accident but, although there were several inquiries, no official version of the president's death was ever presented. In July 1998, Graça Machel married Nelson Mandela.

On our first evening in Maputo, we sat on the hotel's terrace for a while and watched boats swaying gently in the soft night air. Outside, families strolled up and down the waterfront. Inside, when we ordered our dinner, a man at a grand piano began playing 'As Time Goes By', the haunting song popularised by the film classic *Casablanca*. I felt a shiver, almost expecting Ingrid Bergman to glide quietly past us or Humphrey Bogart to appear, cigarette dangling out of the corner of his mouth.

For a while, these scenarios of landmines and terrorists, mysterious plane crashes, a seductively beautiful city, slave trading and European cafes in the damaged heart of Africa had me drifting into a web of past sorrows from which I found it hard to shake free.

—

President Chissano had agreed to our interview. We filmed him in his pale pink palace—one of the most beautiful buildings in Maputo. He was impressive, articulate and charming. He had studied medicine in Portugal, but gave it up to fight in the Mozambican War of Independence where he became a major-general. In the 1960s, in Paris, he represented the Mozambique independence movement (Frelimo), and was known as the soft-spoken diplomat who worked to reconcile radical and moderate Marxist factions of the Frelimo party.

As we talked, he had an air of calm about him. I understood why when he smiled and told me that a few years ago he had decided to learn Transcendental Meditation: 'First I started the practice of Transcendental Meditation myself, then introduced the practice to my close family, my cabinet of ministers, my government officers, my police, my military and 30,000 civilians. The result has been a country of political peace and balance in nature.'

Chissano's faith in meditation and the Maharishi was shown when he negotiated an agreement giving control of twenty million hectares of land in Mozambique—one-quarter of the area of the country—to the Maharishi Heaven on Earth Development Project, which would receive royalties and 80 per cent of the future profits.

ANNE DEVESON

RADIO STAR

Three-careers-at-a-time girl

My broadcasting and writing career is in full swing in 1968.
Source: People

NOBODY is quite sure how she does it, but Anne Deveson combines mothering three young children with a three-sided career as broadcaster, television producer and newspaper columnist.

In private life—what there is of it —she is the wife of broadcaster Ellis Blain, and their children are Jonathon, 7, Georgia, 4, and Joshua, six months.

Five nights a week Anne's voice is heard over 2GB, Sydney, in News-makers. Viewers see her in ATN 7's Beauty and the Beast and her column appears in "The Sun" twice a week.

Workmates think it is a near-miracle that she can fit it all in. Anne puts it this way: "I find the only way is not to nibble, but to work hard while I'm working, and at other times give my whole mind to family affairs. I often work at night, but never at weekends and would not contemplate a 9-to-5 job. I mainly try to stick to things I can prepare at home. Until our third child we managed without a housekeeper."

The voice listeners hear expresses probably the most liberal views heard on air on any Australian commercial network. It never sounds flustered— yet it did once.

It was her first day over 2GB, about four years ago, and with a background of B.B.C. and A.B.C. experience she was naturally eager to launch her new program impressively.

"I was due to come on, live, at 12.30 p.m.," Anne recalls. "At 12.25 I was still cruising around in my car, looking for a parking spot.

"In desperation, I abandoned the car directly under a "No Parking" sign.

"Racing up Hunter Street, I felt the elastic snap on a vital piece of invisible attire, which immediately began to become visible. So I slunk into a quiet doorway, where I could step out of the descending garment, unnoticed. As I did this and poked it into my handbag, I suddenly realised that the quiet doorway was really the entrance to a hotel saloon bar.

"By the time I got to the studio I was three minutes late getting on air. What a dreadful start."

Born in Malaya, Anne was evacuated as a child to Perth when the Japanese struck south. After five years of schooling there she did two years of a science course at London University before journalism called.

In a year wandering about Europe Anne's jobs included working in a toy factory and contributing travel articles to "The New York Times." In Paris, she did a course at the Sorbonne on civilisation.

Back in London—where she was once secretary for a week to Sir Winston Churchill's son, Randolph— she met Ellis Blain. They collaborated on an A.B.C. documentary in Amsterdam on the Dutch psychiatric service, S.O.S. She married Ellis in Melbourne 10 years ago.

Her last overseas trip was to Russia, Poland and Britain for 2GB. Next time she hopes to visit the United States. ●

Sydney, 1972.

The family in Italy, 1972. From left: Josh, 4 years; Georgia, 8 years; Jonathan, 11 years.

Commentary on the findings of the Royal Commission on Human Relationships, 1974. *Reproduced with permission of Ron Tandberg.*

In the Ogaden Desert with World Vision, Ethiopia, 1975. *Source: World Vision Photos*

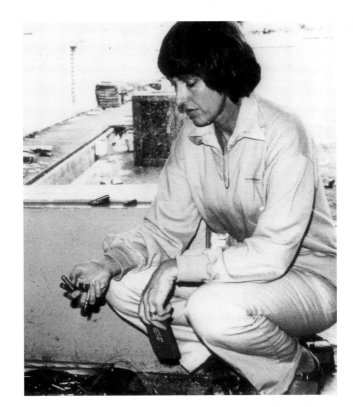

Contemplating the horror of the weaponry left after Idi Amin fled Uganda in 1979. *Source: World Vision Photos*

A newspaper article telling of the horrors in Uganda, 1979.
Source: The Australian

May 16 1979

NEWSMAKERS

ANNE DEVESON . . . home from Uganda with horror stories.

In Idi Amin's den of horrors

Film-maker ANNE DEVESON shuddered yesterday as she recalled the odor of death in IDI AMIN'S infamous torture chamber in Kampala, Uganda.

She said it was the most sickening place she ever saw.

She said: "Up to 200 people were killed there each night. Most were bashed on the head with a hammer and others were tortured, stabbed and strangled.

"Few people survived the appalling place. There were bits of clothing scattered on the floor and boots were lying in the yard."

When she arrived at Sydney Airport yesterday from a five-day tour of Uganda, Miss Deveson said the country was wakening from a nightmare.

She said life in Uganda was beginning to return to normal after Amin's eight-year rule and she noted how things seem to improve each day.

"When we arrived, people were walking around with their eyes downcast, but when we left, they seemed happier and were willing to talk.

"The stores, badly looted during the takeover, were closed on our arrival. They are now beginning to reopen, although supplies are short."

She said milk cost $4 a litre, bread $3 and razor blades $4 — a legacy of Amin's inflation-ridden regime.

Miss Deveson, who made the trip with the communications director of World Vision,

PHILIP HUNT, will make her interviews with leading Ugandans available to television stations.

She said: "The provisional Government wants to bring Amin to trial, but there is little feeling of revenge among the people.

"Amin's spy system permeated every walk of life. Nearly every person we talked with had horror stories to tell.

"For example, a young policeman said he watched hundreds of people being thrown to crocodiles and only escaped himself by tricking Amin's troops.

"Up to 500,000 Ugandans were stabbed, hanged, hammered to death or fed to the crocodiles. The country is now spiritually and economically shattered and aid is desperately needed."
— PETER MORGAN.

Me and my daughter Georgia at an art gallery exhibition opening in 2000.

In 2007, on Chissano's sixty-eighth birthday, he was awarded the inaugural US$5 million dollar Prize for Achievement in African Leadership, awarded by the Mo Ibrahim Foundation.

In conversation and on film, Chissano moved swiftly to his country's problems, all of them related to terrorism and ongoing military support to the terrorists from countries like South Africa and Portugal who were trying to make Mozambique fail. 'We cannot become accustomed to living off handouts,' he said at the beginning of the filmed interview.

> Mozambique cannot be transformed into a country of displaced people, living in relief centres and eating food from abroad. We have maybe sixteen thousand children who don't know the whereabouts of their parents. We have thousands of schools destroyed, and thousands of medical centres. Today we are destitute to a point where our population doesn't have doctors. In education it is the same. And still we have about a million refugees living abroad, and about five million displaced people inside the country.

HUMANITARIAN AID

Renamo operated by moving from village to village, torching houses, burning people alive, beating them to death, strangling, starving, and cutting off limbs, ears, noses and mouths. We filmed as we listened in silence to a small round woman from the village of Booma, who wore a red and black scarf; she folded her arms and looked directly at me, ignoring the tears that were streaking down her face. 'When the bandits arrived they kidnapped people and burned them. My husband and daughter were kidnapped; taken into the bushes and shot. Then they came for me. I was beaten and raped.'

I reached out a hand and she grasped it—strongly—wanting to tell me she would pull through.

The following day we headed north, where life was even harsher. Renamo had just announced it would renew hostilities—'without mercy'. They ambushed a food convoy we were about to join, blew up several trucks and killed twelve people. This meant we were not allowed to stay overnight but had to fly in and out to the refugee camps each day.

We went first to a village that had only just been recaptured from the bandits and where people were severely malnourished. They had been dying at the rate of about fifty a day. Government health workers and a World Vision doctor from the Philippines—Dr Hector Jalaipa—were working together, quickly trying to restore health. This was Stage One of their program. We spent time with two young fathers who were feeding their very small babies in the feeding centre, patiently giving them milk supplements seven times a day. This was culturally atypical, but both young men had finally come to the centre in despair after their wives and other children had died from illness and starvation.

I had expected the village to be burned to the ground, with dead bodies still waiting to be buried, but Dr Jalaipa said that after any attack it was essential to return to normalcy as soon as possible. Two outlying huts had been torched, and these families would share with neighbours. Most people had escaped into the forests.

'And tea is ready,' said Dr Jalaipa, calmly escorting us to the community's long house. Dr Jalaipa was small, slight, with a kindness that radiated from his whole being: his hands extended, his face smiling, and his quiet responses infinitely reassuring.

'Now we visit Stage Two,' said this indefatigable man, who had worked in Ethiopia from 1974 to 1985. He said Ethiopia did not prepare him for the famine he was now witnessing. 'I thought Ethiopia had hardened my heart, but here my heart has broken.'

The savagery of this war still shook him. 'I have seen wounds from hacking with knives that I, a doctor, couldn't look at. Now everyone is much better. In Stage Two, we give seeds, agricultural equipment and a plot of land, so people can be self-sufficient. This is only a staging post, because people nearly all come from other places, sometimes where bandits are still in control.'

Dr Jalaipa told me the intention was to get people back to their own homelands as soon as each region was liberated and made safe. Gradually, order was being achieved as more and more provinces were returned to the government.

The third stage was resettlement. This was represented by a village up in the north of Mozambique which had just harvested its first crop since resettlement and which looked both fertile and secure. We flew into this area, Furuncungo, with the Australian Ambassador and his very pregnant Danish wife. A reception party lined the dirt road leading into the village. Women and children danced and sang. The men slept. 'Men, they always sleep when we have work!' said one of the women.

Our only means of transport was an ancient armoured car. We were told to sit on top but it took ten people to heave me onto its roof, and I nearly fell off the other side, much to the giggles of all the small children who watched, hoping for a fall. When eventually the car rumbled down the road, I clung to the gun turret.

At times, we were filming in heat well into forty degrees Celsius. We would finish late at night, yet I woke at about 5 am each morning with renewed energy, having been fed on goat and rice, rice and goat, and for an occasional treat, goat, rice, chips, spaghetti and boiled potatoes. Most days, we only had one proper meal per day.

Before we left, we spent several days in another community with a thirty-five-year-old Australian nurse, Vivien Wilson, who was a front-line worker in one of the most dangerous parts of Mozambique. As World Vision's Health Officer she was responsible for eleven villages and 40,000 people who lived in the Changara district in the northern province of Tete. She worked with a team of local staff and volunteers, looking after people who had fled Renamo, as well as helping mothers and babies, schoolchildren and pregnant women. Her education programs used music, tribal dancing and puppets. She based much of her work on skills she had developed with the Aboriginal Medical Service in Australia, and at the time of our visit she had trained about a hundred local people to work with her.

Vivien had us lining up with the villagers—a long and straggly row—singing together: 'And we dig our latrines; and we wash our hands, so we're clean, clean, clean. Dig, dig, dig. Wash,

wash, wash. Clean, clean, clean!' At the finish, we all had to leap into the air, shouting, 'Hurrah!'

Vivien was the only white person in this village and lived in a caravan by the river so that if the bandits attacked she could escape into the riverbed. She was a laid-back Queenslander with an atrocious Portuguese accent and a vivid sense of humour. She called the caravan her 'sauna', because the temperatures sometimes rose above forty-five degrees.

Later, when I returned to Australia, I rang her mother, Beryl, in Brisbane to talk about her splendid daughter. 'And I always hoped she'd be a ballet dancer,' she said wistfully.

—

This part of the Changara district was open but quite hilly, with wide blue horizons and rich red soil on which grew bananas, corn and maize. Huts were made of wattle and daub with thatched grass roofs. In many villages they had stopped putting roofs on their huts, because the bandits burned them, setting fire to the whole community. Mostly they all slept out in the open so that if there was an attack they had some chance of running away.

I had decided that if I were attacked, I would hide in the river caves. People would be able to find me later because I would be in among the rushes, playing 'Waltzing Matilda' on my mouth organ. Or if I were unable to run away I would pretend to be a mad white witch, blowing my mouth organ even more discordantly than usual and triumphantly wearing my red clown's nose which, fortunately, I had stuffed into a sock with my mouth organ.

This was not such a daft idea. One of the extraordinary stories in this extraordinary country was the success of a people's army called the White Arms. The White Arms were led by a young man who decided he was sick of his people being butchered by Renamo. First, he set up a health program for eleven villages. Next, he gathered around him a collection of displaced men, women and children, and although they had no weapons, he prepared to resettle those who said they still longed for home.

The White Arms man had been held captive by Renamo for nearly two years, and during that time he studied their psychology. He now drew upon their animistic superstitions to frighten them into running away. His White Arms people went into the forests and prayed to their ancestors for the spirits to come and help them. Then they attacked at night, unarmed but making the most fearsome noise with pots and pans, cow horns and bicycle bells.

I recall asking one young man—he was probably a general— who was clutching a cow horn with bicycle bells at both ends whether the spirits were good or bad.

'Spirits are neither good nor bad,' he said, rubbing his fingers up and down the side of the horn. 'It depends what you do with them.'

15

Resolving Conflict, Keeping Peace

TRYING PEACE

'I declare war on you, Anne Barbara Deveson,' said a gaunt-faced man I scarcely knew. He stood in my kitchen, clutching his duffle coat around him, and leaning with a certain panache against my pantry cupboard.

'I declare war. My cannons are trained on you, from that house over there behind the chimney pots, to your house, here. They will strike you dead.' He picked up a knife and walked up and down. Then he sat on a stool. High up he sat, like a priest robed in black. He said his name was Clayton Pring. His voice sounded like the boom of a cannonball about to knock off my head.

'I declare war,' he repeated. And waited.

'Try peace,' I said. My eyes on the knife.

He laughed, and twiddled his black beret round and round the index finger of his left hand until it looked like a top.

This was the year when we lived in an old bluestone house on the oceanfront of an Adelaide suburb called Grange. It was beautiful in summer and bleak in winter. It was also the house where my son Jonathan became mad. When he was lonely he went forth and multiplied. Night after night he would bring other lost souls to our basement, and in the morning they would drift upstairs to the warmth of our kitchen. On this particular morning, a bitter wind blew sand under our doors and windows. It was cold and I had just made a large pot of tea. The pot was blue, I remember, and it sat in the middle of the kitchen table beside a bunch of freesias.

Pete the Poet was huddled in a corner, shivering. He was fifteen but looked twenty. White face, thin and withdrawn, writing in a battered exercise book that he kept close to his chest. Steve was the other arrival, perched on his customary stool, painstakingly filling in a sheet of graph paper with red ink that matched the surprising brilliance of his hair and beard. He had a childlike innocence and was easily startled. Not so Clayton, the one who declared war. Clayton was older and more sophisticated. I was fearful of Clayton, who said he was Irish, although his accent could metamorphose into a number of other languages, including Arabic. Today, though, he was Irish, his black beret pushed to the back of his head, his manner floating from menace to charm.

'Hide behind the teapot, Anne Barbara Deveson, and you won't be killed,' he crooned.

I nodded and gazed fixedly at the teapot. Its handle was rusty.

'Or you might be killed.' Clayton's voice was suddenly cold.

'Oh, shut up, Clayton,' I said, surprised at my boldness. 'I've told you, I'd rather declare peace.'

He thought about this for a while and then bowed with an exaggerated flourish. 'In that case, madam, we shall declare peace.'

And this we did. We bowed from the waist and shook hands, while Steve continued filling in his squares of graph paper, and Jonathan decided to pour himself a mug of tea. His blond hair fell into his eyes and his hands trembled. I thought the tea would miss the mug. It didn't.

'He's frightened of you,' my son said, helping himself to sugar.

'Me?' said Clayton. 'I'm never frightened.'

'He's frightened.'

If I make this encounter sound coy, don't be fooled. Clayton could be menacing, but formal exchanges made him feel less threatened and therefore less threatening. The fact that we were in a state of war, which then turned to a state of peace, was enough for Clayton. The teapot and I remained safe. And so did Clayton. Had I shouted at Clayton, however, the outcome might have been different. Peace needs the right language to move from conflict to calm. It needs people to listen. It needs respect.

I thought: If a madman can declare peace, why do sane men declare war?

Perhaps old-fashioned wars had some of that same courtesy. Formal. Gentlemanly. Run by the aristocracy, who wore heavy silver armour and rode bold and beautiful horses that whinnied as they pawed the ground.

Aristocrats were rarely slain. If they were toppled from their steeds and lived, the enemy nursed them back to health, then ransomed them for a pretty price. Such romantic pictures of the fallen hero, but such gut-wrenching misery for those who were left behind, lying maimed and bleeding on the ground.

By the time of the Reformation in the sixteenth century, wars became more regimented as the good burghers began to take control. Laws of war were drawn up but only sometimes obeyed. For the wealthy, continuous war became the natural order of things, with a spot of jousting or hunting in between to keep them fit. Peace was regarded as a brief interval between wars, and violence was an accepted way of resolving conflict. Government or the state took care of the big battles. Duels and tournaments were for individual conflicts and were handled by the upper class, the aristocrats.

Johan Galtung, veteran Norwegian peace activist and father of the process of conflict resolution, maintains that only gradually—in the past two hundred years—have political leaders begun to regard peace as a practical or achievable goal. And only gradually have laws become apparent to the public eye, though they are not necessarily enforced or enforceable.

Before the eighteenth century, violence was how conflict was resolved, and winners were believed to have the approval of God. But as the century progressed, significant changes were occurring. Merchants had arrived, and God gave way to the secularisation of society, and the rise of capitalism, markets, bargaining and compromise. Priests joined in.

As well as the growing visibility of laws and the secularisation of society, a third big factor that challenged the older notion of 'might is right' was the growth of democracy, and a growing reluctance on the part of ordinary people to fight the wars of aristocrats. Peace movements grew stronger as citizens became better educated and increasingly reluctant to become involved and, more particularly, to be killed.

'Rather natural, I would say,' says Galtung.

This aversion to being killed was vividly expressed in some of the writings of the First World War. Strong feelings forced their way into words. Consider the shift of mood from death and glory in Tennyson's 'Charge of the Light Brigade' in 1854 to the mocking irony of English biographer and historian Philip Guedalla (1889–1944) in the First World War:

I don't want to join the bloody Army
I don't want to go unto the War,
I want no more to roam,
I'd rather stay at home
Living on the earnings of a whore.
I, Madam, am the civilisation they are fighting for.

But perhaps one of the most poignant shifts in attitudes to war can be found in Rudyard Kipling's lines following the death of his only son, John, in the First World War. Kipling had encouraged—some say bullied—his son to fight, but when the young man was reported missing, then believed killed, Kipling scoured the battlefields, looking in vain for his son, before he wrote: 'If any question why we died, Tell them because our fathers lied.'

During the twentieth century, many attempts were made to explain the reasons for mankind's violence. One of the most interesting was in May 1986, when a group of highly qualified UNESCO scholars from a range of disciplines, addressed issues of violence and war with the following statements:

It is scientifically incorrect to say that we have inherited a tendency to make war from our animal ancestors.

It is scientifically incorrect to say that war or any other violent behaviour is genetically programmed into our human nature.

It is scientifically incorrect to say that in the course of human evolution there has been a selection for aggressive behaviour more than other kinds of behaviour.

It is scientifically incorrect to say that humans have a 'violent brain'. While we do have the neural apparatus to act violently, it is not automatically activated by internal or external stimuli.

It is scientifically incorrect to say that war is caused by instinct or any single motivation.

We conclude that biology does not condemn humanity to war . . . that the same species who invented war is capable of inventing peace.

October 1962

THE CUBAN MISSILE CRISIS

Sometimes I wonder about the relationship between personal violence and the violence of war. Yes, we are all capable of violent behaviour, but this is inflamed and exploited by those whose business is war. How much does patient negotiation and a genuine will to resolve conflict relate to the possibilities of a peaceful outcome? I realise none of this helped Chamberlain in his supplications to Hitler, but there are a growing number of examples where diplomacy and patience have reaped rewards, such as during the Cuban Missile Crisis of October 1962. For fourteen days, the world waited on tenterhooks as US president John F. Kennedy, together with the then first secretary of the Soviet Union, Nikita Khrushchev, desperately argued to avoid nuclear war.

In 1961, the American government had deployed more than one hundred nuclear missiles in Turkey and Italy with the capability of striking Moscow. The Cuban and Soviet governments retaliated by secretly building missile bases in Cuba for a number of nuclear missiles with the ability to strike most of the continental United States. The US armed forces were at their highest state of readiness ever, and if Cuba were invaded, Soviet field commanders were prepared to use battlefield nuclear weapons in defence.

For a fortnight, the world held its breath. That's a cliché; I don't know if or how the world held its breath, but I do remember holding mine. My first child, Jonathan, was just over a year old. By then he had deep dark eyes that gazed into mine, his small fingers clasped my fingers, his warm body nestled into my body, and I loved him with the kind of love I had never thought possible. My arms closed around him fiercely and protectively as I heard the phrases 'surgical strikes' and 'the punishment fits the crime'.

Whose crime? My child had committed no crime. Children in Cuba had committed no crime.

Over breakfast, eating with one hand and feeding Jonathan with the other, I read that Kennedy had interpreted the installation of missiles in Cuba as a move preparatory to a showdown over Berlin. He said: 'A Soviet move on Berlin leaves me only one alternative, which is to fire nuclear weapons—which is a hell of an alternative.'

Phrases like 'gravest issues' were exchanged on the news as US Secretary of State Dean Rush concurred that decision makers could carry the 'mark of Cain' on their brows for the rest of their lives.

I remembered the images from Hiroshima and Nagasaki, the children and babies blinded and burned to death. Khrushchev said he was prepared to remove missiles from Cuba in return for a US promise not to invade the island. Then Khrushchev came back with a further demand: the US must withdraw nuclear missiles and other offensive means from Turkey.

Kennedy's hawks found this unacceptable, but Kennedy's response to them was sharp. 'Most people would regard this as a not unreasonable proposal. I think you are going to find it very difficult to explain why we are going to take hostile military action in Cuba, when he's saying, "If you'll get yours out of Turkey, we'll get ours out of Cuba."'

At the time, the United States had more than 25,000 nuclear weapons in their arsenal. The Soviet Union had nearly half as many. In 1960, Kennedy's predecessor, Dwight Eisenhower, had calculated that if a crisis led either side to fire weapons, all humans in the northern hemisphere could perish.

Throughout the exchanges, Kennedy had a tape recorder installed in an unused part of the White House basement, with wires running to concealed microphones in the Oval Office and Cabinet Room. Reading transcripts of these talks, it is clear how quickly the doves and the hawks began to shake themselves out. In the beginning the hawks appeared the stronger, but gradually the mood shifted as Kennedy took control. The world avoided nuclear war in October 1962, thanks to the forbearance of both Kennedy and Khrushchev.

When I read their exchange, and discern some sense of their anger and frustration, I realise the importance of responsible leadership, of not letting hubris dominate negotiations.

Ireland, 2007

THE TROUBLES

A second, most unexpected peace was won on 8 May 2007 when an historic agreement was signed between Northern Ireland's bitter and longstanding enemies, the Democratic Unionist Party and the republican Sinn Féin.

The vexed history of Ireland dates back to the seventh century, when the English finally succeeded in subduing the island after numerous rebellions. Subsequently, the north became colonised by Scottish and English Protestants, and this set Ulster apart from the rest of Ireland. The north and south grew further apart when industry and manufacturing began flourishing in the north, while the mainly Catholic population in the south suffered from an unequal distribution of land and resources.

By the early twentieth century, the Irish Catholics were demanding home rule and total independence from Britain. This made the Protestants fearful and led to a period of guerrilla warfare between the Irish Republican Army and the British army. A treaty was signed in 1921, but hostilities erupted again in the late 1960s and both sides continued to wage a war of terror known as 'the Troubles'.

Peter Hain, former secretary of state for Northern Ireland, wrote that those who took part in the events of 8 May would have come away with a series of extraordinary images of history in the making. 'It was one of those "it would never happen" days,' said Hain. 'Pictures of Ian Paisley and Sinn Féin leader Gerry Adams meeting together weeks earlier—images which captured world attention because of the level of goodwill between two such sworn enemies.'

I had—and still have—good friends in Northern Ireland: Bertie Trimble, who was the owner and editor of Ulster's *Fermanagh Times*, and his granddaughter Joanna, who took over the newspaper when he retired. They are a generous open-armed family, but if anyone mentions anything about Sinn Féin and Eire, their bitterness is immediate. Peace in Northern Ireland came at a heavy price—3500 dead in nearly four decades.

Yet, despite this, an editorial in the *Times* stated that if one of the longest-running conflicts in European history could be resolved, then there was hope for even the most bitter and seemingly intractable disputes across the globe. As a leader in the *Sydney Morning Herald* pointed out, 'A peace deal or a truce is so easy to break with a bomb or a mass murder—it is humankind's tragedy that commonsense comes so slowly and at so big a price.'

Common sense did come slowly in Northern Ireland. It took generations before the leadership decided the time had come to make compromises. I listened to Gerry Adams when he visited Australia in 2003 to talk about his autobiography, *Hope and History*. It was a sober discussion. The thread that ran through the interview was Adams's expressed belief that there had been enough violence and tragedy. Peace needed the assistance of all sides and beliefs, so those who had successfully forged peace in their own countries—people like Nelson Mandela and Bill Clinton—were invited to contribute.

'It is a wonder to me that we have come through it all,' said Adams. 'We must aim for a just peace. No one ever said that this was going to be easy. But it is the single most important thing that any of us can do at this time in our history.'

—

In June 2012, Queen Elizabeth II made an historic visit to Ireland when, dressed in green, she travelled in an open-top car, and shook hands with former IRA leader Martin McGuinness. McGuinness had been a senior commander in 1979 when a paramilitary group killed the Queen's cousin, Lord Louis Mountbatten, by bombing his boat while he was on holiday in County Sligo. After three decades of bloody sectarian violence, the Queen's handshake was seen by many as an important milestone in Anglo–Irish relations.

Certainly, such an action would have been extremely dangerous during the years of the Troubles. I remember occasional explosions when I visited England, bombing attacks, tension, a feeling of anger snaking its way under the pavements, ready to burst through with gunshot, both sides killing without mercy.

And now the Queen is here, white gloves, hand outstretched to shake: look, children, this is a milestone, remember and put away your sticks and stones.

PLAYING WITH THE ENEMY

Alas, today's wars are still about the business of killing—with an exception. If you happen to be a Trobriand Islander, today's wars are about cricket. Sometime during the late nineteenth century, newly arrived British Methodist missionaries found the ritualised form of intertribal war practised by the Trobrianders was not only barbaric, but black magic had usurped the place of God. In its place, missionary William Gilmore suggested warfare with spears should be replaced by cricket with bats and balls.

The Trobrianders agreed; perhaps they were sick of killing, or perhaps cricket was more fun. The game was quickly adapted to Trobriand culture by expanding the number of players, introducing ritualised dancing and chanting, and modifying the bats and balls. The game evolved and continues to evolve. Fifty men per side; palm fronds or yams for counting the score; bats, balls and stumps carved out of wood; and cricketing clothes made from the bark of a betelnut tree. On the morning of a game, the warriors wake early, put on their war paint and battle-dress, and dance in line to the host village. Dances often have special meaning, including sexual innuendo and erotic themes, while the spectacle includes tribal totems and advertising slogans. The game usually lasts for two days, and rather than giving away trophies, games end with feasts provided by the host chief. The home team is always the winner. Trobrianders believe that human nature can be both good and evil, and elders are revered; they are not allowed to play cricket, but they can keep the score.

As a revered elder, I am glad I am not allowed to play cricket. I once played with an Australian women's media team against the British women's cricket team. I trod on my own wicket, dropped a catch, fell over and was only able to bowl underarm. Everyone was kind to me, which made matters worse.

But I have been thinking about how and why cricket so successfully replaced war in the Trobriand Islands, and wonder how much was due to the fact that the game is fun and competitive, yet operates within agreed rules and rituals and thus offers a safety net for whatever combat might arise.

Then there's that well-known story that unfolded one Christmas Eve in the First World War. It was cold, and soldiers shivered in the trenches as they faced each other across a dark silent stretch of no-man's-land. German soldiers were in one line of trenches; French, English and Scottish soldiers in the opposite line. They were all stamping their feet, trying to keep warm. Fighting had temporarily ceased when a young German soldier spontaneously began singing 'Stille Nacht'—'Silent Night'. Hesitantly, other voices joined in as, one by one, all the soldiers lay down their arms, left their trenches and walked into the dark of no-man's-land to exchange gifts, pray together, sing together and even play soccer.

The war didn't end because this happened, but neither has its telling ended—and this is the memory we need to hold close whenever we are confronted with the stupidity of war, and the healing power of peace.

'The world does not have to be the way it is,' writes South American novelist and playwright Ariel Dorfman over and over again. 'The world does not have to be the way it is.' Try reading it and saying it. Do not stop until it becomes a part of you. 'The world does not have to be the way it is.'

PEACE BROKERS

So much has happened since Johan Galtung first pioneered his work on peace and conflict studies in Oslo in 1959. Ten years later he was appointed to the world's first Chair in Peace and Conflict Studies at the University of Oslo. Since then, not just the notion of conflict resolution but its skills and practices have spread around the world, from those working with children in their early school years to teach them how to resolve their problems instead of hitting each other, to anyone or any organisation that wishes to become more skilled in the practice of conflict resolution. Some courses are given by specialists in preventive law; others might specialise in indigenous disputes, wills and estates, industry schemes, commercial and business management . . . It's almost a case of look for what you want and you'll find it.

During the miners' strike at Lonmin's Marikana mine in South Africa in 2012, mediation and arbitration commissioners worked tirelessly to help broker peace.

At one stage, a few years earlier, it felt as if there were a zeitgeist in the air. I recall having afternoon tea with a six-year-old whose parents were squabbling. It was about something relatively minor, but the dispute clearly disturbed the little girl. 'Come along, you two,' she said, as if she were eighty-six years old rather than six. 'I think it's time you stopped quarrelling and had a nice cup of tea so you can be friends again.'

She was intuitively right; being there, and listening to both sides of a conflict, however big or small, is an intrinsic part of conflict resolution—but how many times have we heard world leaders refusing to meet, let alone talk?

JUST WAR?

> When thou shalt besiege a city a long time, in making war against it to take it, thou shalt not destroy the trees thereof by forcing an axe against them: for thou mayest eat of them, and thou shalt not cut them down (for the tree of the field is man's life). (Deuteronomy 20:19–20)

Whenever I read about a *just war* and the *laws of war*, I feel conflicted. In one mood, I think how excellent the concept of having laws to govern our wars is. In another mood, it seems ludicrous to think that we can actually control something as unpredictable and violent as war; at these times, it seems as though the very phrase 'just war' is an oxymoron. At the same time as we are talking about how to save civilians, we are also killing people in ways that sometimes make Jack the Ripper seem like Snow White. Remember Abu Ghraib? The torture, psychological and sexual; the rape, sodomy, and murder of prisoners by US military police during the war against Iraq? Or when we claimed there was absolutely no use of torture in our warfare, and certainly nothing like rendition?

I learned about *just wars* when we were filming in Somalia, when warlords were fighting US marines in circumstances that were supposed to guarantee the safety of civilians. We stayed at a small hotel where the first thing we were taught by our Somali guide was not to tuck our sheets under our mattresses because, should armed Somali soldiers enter our room, it was essential to roll immediately out of our blankets and onto the floor *without making a noise* and then hide under our beds, also *without making a noise.*

I said I thought the soldiers were supposed to be protecting us.

'They are,' said our guide. 'But we do not always do what we are told.'

I did not expect to be given hot milk and honey as a bedtime treat, but neither had I quite grasped the fact that we were in a war zone and risked being killed. I also came to realise that a global human rights culture doesn't necessarily promise the practice of human rights.

I look at a book called *The Laws of War: A comprehensive collection of primary documents on international laws governing armed conflict* and read (1) that the laws of war have always been an 'unorganized' legal system, and (2) wars of annihilation—in which one group is trying to annihilate another—do not lend themselves to litigation. Wars of control are more manageable.

'Just war' theory has two sets of criteria. The first establishes *jus ad bellum*, the right to go to war; the second establishes *jus in bello*, right conduct within war. A third category has now been added—*jus post bellum*—which governs the justice of war termination and peace agreements, as well as the prosecution of war criminals.

Just war theorists are said to combine a moral abhorrence of war with a readiness to accept that war may sometimes be necessary. Just war theories are attempts 'to distinguish between justifiable and unjustifiable uses of organized armed forces'; they try 'to conceive of how the use of arms might be restrained, made more humane, and ultimately directed towards the aim of establishing lasting peace and justice'.

The notions are grand ones, but their execution is problematic. When we rely on Kalashnikovs or bombs to protect both us and our humanity we are doomed to failure. There is no justice in blowing up a child, or killing a nineteen-year-old soldier who has no say in how or why he fights.

The war in Somalia wasn't a just war, but I wonder if there are any truly just wars? The war fought against Germany from 1939 to 1945 did seem to me a just war, in its need to halt a tyrant and a killer. *But it was not just in its execution.* From the Indian epic of Mahabharata to Christian theories of the just war, attempts have been made to define 'just causes'—such as retaliation for breach of a treaty—and proportionality (for example, chariots cannot attack cavalry, only other chariots). War must occur for a good and just purpose rather than for self-gain. Just war theorists even attempt to conceive how the use of arms might be restrained, made more humane, and ultimately directed towards the aim of establishing lasting peace and justice. But just wars often put their faith in warriors, the fighters whose military code requires them to continue fighting and to kill, and the humanitarians who nod their heads considering how to make drones more humane—to play music as they kill? Probably they are already programmed.

1997

A TREATY TO BAN LANDMINES

Many people consider campaigns for disarmament a hopeless cause, given the vested interests ranged against it. The international campaign to ban landmines is one of the most striking examples. Landmines kill indiscriminately long after war is over. Children are frequently the victims. The immorality of using such weapons is obvious, yet for too long this has been disregarded. So many attempts have been made to ratify UN control; so many countries have attempted to block it.

I was familiar with landmines ever since I started filming in Africa in 1974. I'd seen the carnage suffered by children in Mozambique. In Rwanda I had heard an Italian war surgeon swear softly to himself while he amputated the leg of a small boy who had trodden on a landmine earlier that day. The surgeon told me that this child's father had already been killed by mines and now he, the eldest son, would no longer be able to help his family with growing food—both to eat and to sell.

South-East Asia was another area particularly savaged by mines. Bomb craters in Laos are the stark legacy of a campaign that saw more than two million bombs dropped by the United States. Millions of unexploded mines infest the country. Yet in 1955, a UN conference dedicated to controlling inhumane weapons ended in a failure to agree on tighter controls over landmines.

In 1992, along came a woman called Jody Williams, strong, vibrant and determined, an academic and peace activist who drew together a group of non-government organisations to help form the International Campaign to Ban Landmines—ICBL. She began with a staff of one—herself—and worked tirelessly with governments, UN bodies and the Red Cross to build an international organisation eventually numbering 1300 NGOs in ninety countries. The organisation achieved the Mine Ban Treaty in 1997—known as the Ottawa Treaty—banning the use, production, stockpiling, and transfer of anti-personnel mines.

According to the ICBL's website, by 2012, 80 per cent of the world's countries have agreed to be bound by the treaty, and the ICBL continues to work for a world free of anti-personnel mines and cluster munitions.

Jody Williams and the ICBL received a Nobel Peace Prize in 1997 for their work In 2006, they joined with two other Nobel Peace Laureates to establish the Nobel Women's Initiative to promote the efforts of women all around the world working for peace with justice and equality. Aung San Suu Kyi is an honorary member.

This is an inspiring story. It shows that if a very few determined people get together they can achieve great things.

17 December 2010

ARAB SPRING

On 17 December 2010, a young unemployed graduate and breadwinner for his siblings and widowed mother, Tunisian Mohamed Bouazizi, was selling vegetables when police seized his goods and cart because he did not have a permit. He was then slapped by a police officer and publicly humiliated. He protested by setting fire to himself, and died. This act provoked other young Tunisians to protest in a wave of demonstrations, known as the Arab Spring, that spread across the Arab world.

Rulers have been forced from power in Tunisia, Egypt, Libya and Yemen; major protests have been staged in Algeria, Iraq, Jordan, Kuwait, Morocco and Sudan. At the time of writing, a fierce civil war continues in Syria, where thousands have been killed.

An article by Lisa Anderson, president of the American University in Cairo, reminds us that the Arab Spring story is not about globalisation or how activists used technology (as many claimed), but about how and why these particular countries revolted. The demonstrations shared a common call for dignity and responsive government, while the revolutions of Tunisia, Libya and Egypt reflected divergent economic grievances and social dynamics—legacies of diverse encounters with modern Europe and decades under unjust regimes.

16

Looking Back, Looking Forward

When I was at boarding school in Australia, every Sunday we would open our mouths wide and chorus our supreme confidence in holding dominion over the earth and all its creatures. We were God's head prefects, vastly superior to all other forms of life. In the western tradition, our science had given us faith in a world that was ordered, predictable and neatly divisible into its component parts—a Newtonian view that had altered little since the seventeenth century.

One of the most profound discoveries in my lifetime occurred, therefore, when scientists began to examine how even the smallest of changes in any given system could produce unexpected and dramatically magnified results. These theories were popularised by New York science writer James Gleick, whose 1988 book *Chaos* described how butterflies stirring the air today in China might well affect the weather somewhere else in the world. Since reading this, I sometimes think when birds restlessly chatter on the telegraph wires, or the tide pulls crazily to one side of the beach creating dangerous little whirlpools, that, despite forecasts for fine weather, those butterflies in Beijing might be responsible for storm clouds over the coast where I live. Chaos theory is mysterious and humbling stuff, and to me was a revelation into the power of interconnectedness—and into the possibilities for promoting peace.

It flashed through my mind that had my father still been alive, and I'd asked him what he thought of my ideas about peace, he'd have told me that an idealist was ever bound for disappointment.

'Bah!' I thought with affection, refraining from stomping up and down the hallway, which had been his usual method of defence. 'But what could happen if we put as much effort into making peace as we do into making war?'

'You'd lose the lot,' my father would have grumbled.

Yet in my eight decades I've seen massive resources—funds, materials, lives—lost in waging war, with consequences for nations, peoples and families just like my own. It is not only a nation's young men who suffer disproportionately the horrors of war; often women, unarmed civilians and the innocent suffer as much or more than the soldiers persuaded by ideas of 'honour' into killing and dying. The consequences for everyone go way beyond the knowable or measurable; beyond lost lives and limbs, destruction of homes, dispossession and displacement, environments poisoned, economies wrecked. Even exposure to warfare can cause lasting damage—as I witnessed in my own father, after his experiences in escaping the Japanese attack on Singapore. Post-traumatic stress, such as my father suffered, is an effect of war only recently 'discovered' and treated, though it must have always existed. Countless families have had to endure such effects long after the wars have ended.

A peaceful world can exist only if we recognise the inter-dependent nature of humankind. As with all relationships, our future lies in collaboration and understanding rather than coercion and exploitation. This, I believe, is realism rather than unachievable idealism.

Scholar and historian Michael Ignatieff says we are scarcely aware of the extent to which our narrative of compassion and moral commitment has been transformed since the end of the Second World War by a shared culture of human rights.

'*Doucement, doucement*—gently, gently,' I recall again the young French lieutenant as he watched his men throw corpses into a large yellow disposal truck after the Rwandan genocide. 'These are human beings—they could have been your mother or your father. *Doucement, doucement.*'

Peace is not just the ending of war nor the space between wars; it lies in the joy of ordinary living, spending time with friends and families. A few powerful individuals can blow such precious peace away.

Enormous changes *have* occurred as people around the world have reconsidered traditions and used democratic voices to bring about social change—the development of peace movements, the evolution of universal human rights, the feminist revolution, and the extraordinary expansion of communications technology that now spreads ideas across the world in ways that were previously unimaginable.

One person's lifetime is a useful frame in which to explore change, and reflecting on mine has helped me to understand the scale and significance of changes of the last fifty years in the culture of peace. When I was visiting Adelaide recently—that most civilised of cities—I sat on a hilltop early one summer evening, looking down at a sparkling of lights, and reflected on the change in attitudes. I remembered news footage of young servicemen who openly declared to TV cameras that they didn't want to go to war with Iraq, and of others who were ready to go but respected the rights of people who opposed the war, and I heard that these young servicemen were neither punished nor reprimanded. I recalled hearing of an Australian bomber pilot, who was flying with two American planes in a bombing mission over Baghdad, turning back when he feared his bombs might falls on civilians—a brave action for which I believe no disciplinary action was taken. Similarly, 'refuseniks' from the Israeli air force, who refused to fly bombers over Iraq, were merely reprimanded. It reminded me of the First World War, when conscientious objectors to conscription and fellow pacifists were handed white feathers, a symbol of cowardice, and some were even court-martialled and imprisoned. Nowadays, pacifists are interviewed in popular magazines.

In the Second World War, too, graffiti found in a US army latrine said it pithily:

Soldiers who wish to be a hero
Are practically zero,
But those who wish to be civilians,
Jesus, they run into millions.

Attitudes have changed because the public today have access to truer reports of war, and a better understanding of the complex factors that give rise to war. To wage peace as passionately as we have in the past waged wars, we must more fully know and understand the forces leading to conflict, and the interests vested in mongering war—ideological, political and commercial. We can then dedicate equivalent strategy and resources to preventing war and to waging peace.

Communication has always been a key factor in the waging of wars—from nationalistic propaganda to media censorship and embedded war correspondents. The general public has rarely had access to objective or truthful accounts of the causes or consequences of wars that we have been asked to endure. No parliamentary debates approved Australia's involvement in the dishonourable war against Iraq. Weeks and months passed before we realised the trickery about those 'weapons of mass destruction'—thanks to Dr Hans Blix, who was awarded the 2005 Nobel Peace Prize.

In today's world, fast, uncensored internet and mobile communication can bring about political revolution, as the Arab Spring has shown. Will this new media more effectively 'speak truth to power', and will it be able to galvanise efforts for conflict resolution and even peace? Or will it, in some countries, be suppressed and its writers silenced by imprisonment or even torture?

We have already come a long way in developing strategies to promote peace and contain conflict. Peoples, nations, the international community, have in recent times devised an impressive range of protocols to deal with every stage of potential or actual conflict. An exhaustive list would be far too long, but consider these developments: rules of war, human rights safeguards, promotion of intercultural and interfaith understanding, peace accords, protocols for conflict resolution, disarmament agreements, prohibitions against torture, independent agencies such as Red Cross and Red Crescent, truth and reconciliation commissions, international courts of justice and retribution for war criminals, international interventions and peace-keeping forces. Each building block of each such institution has been set in place by people who believe in waging peace—activists, intellectuals, communicators, professionals, progressive leaders. Their achievements would shock the warlords, kings, popes, sultans and generals of yore, for such institutions would threaten the maintenance of their power.

The long, long list of courageous human beings who have believed in the possibility of peace continues to inspire my optimism. Buddha and Jesus may have been a bit ahead of their time with their agenda of compassion and peace, but countless other ordinary mortals have promoted such ideas since: philosophers like Rousseau and Kant, Quakers like William Penn, scientists like Albert Einstein and Linus Pauling, leaders like Gandhi, Martin Luther King, the Dalai Lama and Nelson Mandela, singers like Bob Dylan, Joan Baez and John Lennon. And the contribution made to making and keeping the peace by women, so rarely acknowledged, is now becoming recognised: women like Betty Williams and Mairead Corrigan of the Community of Peace People, a Northern Ireland peace movement, Leymah Gbowee of Liberia, and journalist Tawakol Karman of Yemen, the youngest woman to win a Nobel Prize.

—

Peace . . . the deep well of truth of what we all want, each man, each woman, each child on this earth; that the small space that surrounds our fragile bodies be respected; that our right to some minimal territoriality or identity or autonomy be afforded recognition by those who have the power to smash and invade it.

Ariel Dorfman

We live in an interdependent world—the air we breathe, the water we drink, the food we eat—even the germs that can kill us, all these we share, just as we must share the oil we need for power.

We need to recognise how much we have achieved, and how much more must be done. One of our greatest responsibilities lies with looking after our children who, one day, will hold stewardship of this perplexing, yet magical world. As I write, I can hear young voices laughing, dogs barking, people talking. I can smell the sea, and enjoy the sound of leaves scuttering in the breeze.

How we nurture instead of destroy the planet on which we live is inextricably bound up with how we secure a just and peaceful world. As R. Buckminster Fuller—that inventive and visionary American thinker of the 1960s—put it, 'Either wars are obsolete, or men are'.

Notes

Chapter 1—Growing Up with War

'All things bright and beautiful'
'All Things Bright and Beautiful', words Mrs Cecil Frances Alexander, 1848.

'Onward, Christian soldiers'
'Onward, Christian Soldiers', words Sabine Baring-Gould, 1865.

Chapter 2—Journey

'It is an ancient Mariner'
Samuel Taylor Coleridge, 'The Rime of the Ancient Mariner', *Poetry of the English-Speaking World*, Readers Union with William Heinemann, London, 1957, p. 530.

Chapter 3—Malaya

'An hour earlier, the Japanese offensive'
Margaret Shennan, *Out in the Midday Sun, The British in Malaya 1800–1966*, John Murray, London, 2000, pp. 222–3.

'As I turned over and twisted in bed'
Winston S. Churchill, *The Grand Alliance*, Cassell, London, 1950, p. 551.

'You can take it from me'
Muriel C. Reilly, 'Diary of her Experiences in Singapore and of her Escape to Australia', dated March 1942, BAM XII/24, p. 1 (unpublished).

'People in Penang are still stunned'
Malayan Gazette, editorial, 16 December 1941.

'Allies with our servants and cooks'
Ian Morrison, *Malayan Postscript*, Faber, London, 1942, p. 228.

'The British and the Asiatics'
Ian Morrison, ibid.

'I make it quite clear that Australia'
Prime Minister John Curtin, *Herald*, 27 December 1941.

'Either we were crazy'
Margaret Shennan, *Out in the Midday Sun: The British in Malaya 1880–1966*, John Murray, London, 2000.

'The fall of Singapore'
'Singapore was the Dunkirk of Australia', *Canberra Times*, 17 February 1942, p. 3, http://nla.gov.au/nla.news-article2564512, accessed 15 January 2013.

Chapter 4—Becoming Refugees

'simply entitled *Resilience*'
Anne Deveson, *Resilience*, Allen & Unwin, Sydney, 2003.

Chapter 5—Escaped

'It seemed as if the streets were paved with heads'
'All Over Bar the Shouting', *TES Newspaper*, 22 April, 2005, http://www.tes.co.uk/article.aspx?storycode=2093122, accessed 15 January 2013.

'We have never seen a greater day than this'
Alexander Heffner, 'The Origins of His Oratory', *Wall Street Journal*, New York, 13 August 2012, http://online.wsj.com/article/SB1000087239639044 4226904577558932167545946.html, accessed 15 January 2013.

Chapter 6—Repatriated

'To walk through the ruined cities of Germany'
George Orwell, 'Future of a Ruined Germany', *Observer*, 8 April 1945.

'I wish I loved the human race'
Professor Sir Walter Alexander Raleigh (1861–1922), 'Wishes of an Elderly Man', wished at a garden party, June 1914.

'The prospect for the human race'
Bertrand Russell, 'The Bomb and Civilisation', *Glasgow Forward*, 1945, vol. 39, no. 33, p. 3.

'Winston Churchill described the plan'
Hugh Wilford, 'Should We Say Thank You?', *London Review of Books*, 2009.

'Real power is about generosity'
Eve Ensler, 'The New Paradigm We Hold Within' in *Stop the Next War Now: Effective Responses to Violence and Terrorism*, M. Benjamin and J. Evans (eds), Inner Ocean Publishing Inc., Makawao, Hawaii, 2005, pp. 29–30.

'There will be no peace for the Allies'
Louis Fischer, *The Life of Mahatma Ghandi*, HarperCollins, London, 1997, p. 409.

Chapter 9—Missing Peace

'For after grete war cometh good pees'
Aesop, 'The Hares and the Frogs', *The Fables of Aesop, as first printed by William Caxton in 1484, with those of Avian, Alfonso and Poggio, now again edited and induced by Joseph Jacobs*, 1494/1889, Westminster/London, p. 43.

'on 9 November 1938, also known as Krystallnacht'
Krystallnacht, or the Night of Broken Glass, an anti-Jewish pogrom in
Nazi Germany and Austria, 9–10 November 1938.

'My blood was boiling'
George W. Bush, *Decision Points*, Crown Publishing Group, New York,
2010, p. 128.

'According to French academic, Dominique Reynié'
Alex Callinicos, 'Anti-war Protests Do Make a Difference', *Socialist
Worker*, 19 March 2005, www.socialistworker.co.uk/articles.php?article-
id=6067, accessed 1 November 2007.

'The strength and size of the demonstrations'
Patrick E. Tyler, 'A New Power in the Streets', *New York Times*,
17 February 2003.

'the world being sentenced to life imprisonment'
Wole Soyinka, *Climate of Fear*, Random House Publishing Group, New
York, 2005, p. 24.

Chapter 10—So Why War?

'no theorist, and no commander'
Carl von Clausewitz, *On War (Vom Krieg)*, M. Howard and P. Paret (eds),
Princeton University Press, New Jersey, 1984 (1832), p. 137.

'Why do millions of people'
Leo Tolstoy, *War and Peace*, translated by Louise and Aylmer Maude,
Simon & Schuster, New York, 1942, p. 1359.

'In all history there is no war'
Leo Tolstoy, ibid.

'Blazing rockets'
Louis de Broglie, A General Survey of the Scientific Work of Albert
Einstein, in Physics' in *Albert Einstein*, P. Schilpp (ed.), Harper and Row,
New York, 1959, p. 110 .

'The release of atom power'
Albert Einstein, quoted in *New Statesman*, 16 April 1965. Cited in
Nicholas Humphrey, *Leaps of Faith: Science, Miracles, and the Search for
Supernatural Consolation*, Springer-Verlag, New York, 1999, p. 25.

'Biographer John Simon writes how Einstein's egalitarian streak
John J. Simon, 'Albert Einstein, Radical: A Political Profile', *Monthly
Review*, vol. 57, no. 1, May 2005, http://monthlyreview.org/2005/05/01/
albert-einstein-radical-a-political-profile, accessed 15 January 2013.

'Dear Professor Freud'
Albert Einstein, Sigmund Freud, Fritz Moellenhoff, Anna Moellenhoff,
*Why War? The Correspondence Between Albert Einstein and Sigmund
Freud*, Chicago Institute for Psychoanalysis, 1933.

'As long as all international conflicts'
Albert Einstein, *Nord-Ost*, 20 April 1932.

'no insight into the dark places'
Albert Einstein, ibid.

'Dear Mr Einstein'
Sigmund Freud, September 1932, ibid.

'What progress we are making'
Epilogue, *Young Dr Freud: A Film by David Grubin*, http://www.pbs.org/
youngdrfreud/pages/epilogue.htm, accessed 15 January 2013.

'Doctor, a human being'
Michihiko Hachiya, *Hiroshima Diary: The Journal of a Japanese Physi-
cian, August 6–September 30, 1945*, translated by Warner Wells MD,
University of North Carolina Press, 1955, p. 108.

'There is always a way'
John J. Simon, ibid.

'I can see a future for Palestine'
Albert Einstein, in John J. Simon, ibid.

'There lies before us'
Albert Einstein in 'Albert Einstein, Radical: A Political Profile', *Monthly
Review*, vol. 57, no.1, May 2005.

'revolutionary'
Albert Einstein, ibid.

Chapter 11—War's Just Human Nature

'There will always be wars'
Peter Cosgrove, *Weekend Australian Magazine* interview, 5–6 September
2009.

'But we weren't like the Good Samaritan'
'Private Harry Patch' (Obituary), *Telegraph*, 25 July 2009, http://www.tele-
graph.co.uk/news/obituaries/military-obituaries/army-obituaries/
5907316/Private-Harry-Patch.html, accessed 15 January 2013.

'Politicians who took us to war'
Harry Patch with Richard van Emden, *The Last Fighting Tommy: The Life
of Harry Patch*, Bloomsbury, London, 2007, p. 188.

'Africa scared me'
Robert Ardrey, *African Genesis: A Personal Investigation Into the Animal
Origins and Nature of Man*, Dell, New York, 1967, p. 188.

'Leakey agrees that while our ancestors'
Richard E. Leakey and Roger Lewin, *Origins Reconsidered: In Search of
What Makes Us Human*, Anchor, New York, 1993, p. xvii.

'Modern studies of the behaviour of wild animals'
Boyce Rensberger, APF newsletter, 1973, Boyce R. and Alicia Patterson
Foundation award winner with support from the LSB Leakey Foundation, credited to APF and LSB L. Foundation, http://en.wikipedia.org/
wiki/Killer_ape_theory.

'Some kill one another's infants'
Robert M. Sapolsky, 'A Natural History of Peace', *New York Times*,
2 January 2006, http://www.nytimes.com/cfr/international/
20060101faessay_v85n1_sapolsky.html, accessed 15 January 2013.

'And boy, is this ever a different ape'
Robert Sapolsky, ibid.

'We need to build on that'
Frans de Waal, 'Frans de Waal: Moral Behavior in Animals' at TEDx-Peachtree, filmed 2011, posted April 2012, http://www.ted.com/talks/frans_de_waal_do_animals_have_morals.html, accessed 22 January 2013.

'Ethnic cleansing happened . . . this community is making progress'
William Shawcross, *Deliver us from Evil*, Bloomsbury, London, p. 375.

'Folk wisdom generalises'
C. Eisenegger, M. Naef, R. Snozzi, M. Heinrichs and E. Fehr, 'Prejudice and truth about the effect of testosterone on human bargaining behaviour', *Nature*, no. 463, December 2009, pp. 356–9.

'The preconception that testosterone'
Christoph Eisenegger, 'Testosterone Won't Make You Aggro: Study', ABC Science / AFP Wednesday, 9 December 2009, http://www.abc.net.au/science/articles/2009/12/09/2766165.htm, accessed 15 January 2013.

'It appears that it is not testosterone'
Michael Naef, ibid.

'If you take out uncovered meat'
Sheik Taj Din al-Hilali, reported in Richard Kerbaj 'Muslim leader blames women for sex attacks', *Australian*, 26 October 2006, http://www.theaustralian.com.au/news/nation/muslim-leader-blames-women-for-sex-attacks/story-e6frg6nf-1111112419114, accessed 15 January 2013.

Chapter 12—So What Is Peace?

'a period of cheating'
Ambrose Bierce, *The Devil's Dictionary*, The World Publishing Co., Cleveland and New York, 1911, p. 248 ('Peace, n.').

'Peace is not an absence of war'
Benedictus de Spinoza, *Volume 1 of The Chief Works of Benedict de Spinoza*, Bell, Michigan, 1887, p. 314.

'I have made a ceaseless effort'
Benedictus de Spinoza, ibid.

'The deep well of truth'
Ariel Dorfman, 'A Different Drum', *Guardian*, 11 January 2003, http://
www.guardian.co.uk/books/2003/jan/11/fiction.politics, accessed
15 January 2013.

'in the run-up to the Iraq war'
Jane Mayer, 'Contract Sport: What did the Vice-President do for Halliburton?', *The New Yorker*, 16 February 2004, http://www.newyorker.com/
archive/2004/02/16/040216fa_fact?currentPage=all, accessed 16 January
2013.

'Kant became one of the first to argue'
Immanuel Kant *The Philosophy of Kant*, Carl J. Friedrich (ed.), Modern
Library, New York, 1949, p. 123.

'a woman's view of peace and war'
Elise Boulding, *Cultures of Peace: The Hidden Side of History*, Syracuse
University Press, Syracuse, NY, 2000, p. 15.

'The dynamic depends on history'
Andrew Bacevich, *London Review of Books*, vol. 27, no. 5, 3 March 2005,
pp. 25-6.

'It has turned out to be a beautiful'
Raja Shehadeh, *When the Bulbul Stopped Singing*, Profile Books, London,
2003, p. 42

'Brute force can never subdue'
The Dalai Lama, 'My Vision of a Compassionate Future', *Washington Post*,
21 October 2007, http://www.washingtonpost.com/wp-dyn/content/
article/2007/10/17/AR2007101701140.html, accessed 16 January 2013.

'the great Australian silence'
W.E.H. Stanner, *After the Dreaming: Black and White Australians—An
Anthropologist's View*, Australian Broadcasting Commission, 1969, p. 27.

Chapter 1 3—Rights and Relationships

'The women of the world'
Simone de Beauvoir, *The Second Sex*, translated by Constance Borde and
Sheila Malovany-Chevallier, Random House, London 1949/2009, p. 289.

'worthless circus'; 'a synonym for futility'; 'a giant talk-back radio show';
'an attempt to pry'; 'an extraordinary achievement'; 'the most exhaustive
study'; 'I went to scoff'
Quoted in Anne Deveson, *Australians at Risk*, Cassell Australia, Sydney
and Melbourne, 1978, p. 4.

'Some night staff change beds'
Final Report of the Royal Commission on Human Relationships, Australian
Government Publishing Services, Canberra, 1977.

'These women are being treated for anxiety'
Final Report of the Royal Commission on Human Relationships, ibid.

Chapter 14—Into Africa

'Every time we stepped outside the wire'
Letters to the editor, *Sydney Morning Herald*, 16 December 2005. State-
ment from a forward scout in the 4th Battalion RAR/NZ regiment in
Vietnam, 1969: name G.E. Barr, ex–Royal Australian Regiment.

'The great grey-green, greasy Limpopo'
Rudyard Kipling, *Just So Stories for Little Children*, MacMillan and Co,
London, 1916, p. 58.

Chapter 15—Resolving Conflict, Keeping Peace

'only gradually—in the past two hundred years—have political leaders'
Johan Galtung speaking in 'Conflict Resolution', Rear Vision, ABC Radio
National, 13 August 2006, http://www.abc.net.au/radionational/programs/
rearvision/conflict-resolution/3340128, accessed 22 January 2013.

'Rather natural, I would say'
Johan Galtung, ibid.

'I don't want to join the bloody Army'
Philip Guedalla, *Voices from the Great War*, ed. Peter Vansittart Cape
London, 1981, p. 56.

'If any question why we died'
Rudyard Kipling, 'Common Form' from 'Epitaphs' in *The Years Between*,
Doubleday, New York, 1919, p. 137.

'a group of highly qualified UNESCO scholars'
Seville Statement of Violence, convened by Spanish National Committee
for UNESCO, Seville, Spain, 16 May 1986.

'It was one of those "it would never happen" days'
Peter Hain, 'Peacemaking in Northern Ireland: A Model for Conflict
Resolution?', speech by Peter Hain, then Secretary of State for Northern
Ireland, Chatham House, London, 12 June 2007, Belfast: Northern Ireland
Office, p. 2.

'if one of the longest-running conflicts'
In Peter Hain's speech, ibid.

'A peace deal or truce'
Editorial, 'Eventually Others Will Follow Northern Ireland's Path to
Peace', *Sydney Morning Herald*, 3 February 2007, http://www.smh.com.au/
news/editorial/eventually-others-will-follow-northern-irelands-path-to-
peace/2007/02/02/1169919528849.html?page=fullpage, accessed
16 January 2013.

'It is a wonder to me'
Gerry Adams, *A Farther Shore: Ireland's Long Road to Peace*, Random
House, New York, 2005, p. 5.

'The world does not have to be the way it is'
Ariel Dorfman, 'Conclusion As Manifesto: Imagining a Possible Peace' in
Other Septembers, Many Americas: Selected Provocations, 1980–2004,
Seven Stories Press, New York, 2004, p. 253.

'that the laws of war'
*The Laws of War: A Comprehensive Collection of Primary Documents on
International Laws Governing Armed Conflict*, Michael Reisman and
Chris T Antoniou (eds), Vintage Books, New York, p. xvii.

'the Arab Spring story is not about globalisation'
Lisa Anderson, 'Demystifying the Arab Spring: Parsing the Differences
Between Tunisia, Egypt, and Libya', *Foreign Affairs*, May/June 2011, http://
www.foreignaffairs.com/articles/67693/lisa-anderson/demystifying-the-
arab-spring, accessed 16 January 2013.

Chapter 16—Looking Back, Looking Forward

James Gleick, Chaos: Making a New Science, Viking Penguin, New York, 1987.

'the extent to which our narrative of compassion'
Michael Ignatieff, *The Warrior's Honor: Ethnic War and the Modern Conscience*, Vintage, London, 1999, p. 8.

'Peace . . . the deep well of ruth of what we all want'
Ariel Dorfman, 'A Different Drum', *The Guardian*, 11 January 2003, http://www.guardian.co.uk/books/2003/jan/11/fiction.politics, accessed 15 January 2013.

'Either wars are obsolete, or men are'
R. Buckminster Fuller, as quoted in Calvin Thomas, 'In the Outlaw Area' *The New Yorker*, 8 January 1966, herehttp://www.newyorker.com/archive/1966/01/08/1966_01_08_035_TNY_CARDS_000279141, accessed 22 January 2013.

Acknowledgements

This is a book that grew over many years, punctuated by illness and inspired by the wisdom of my friends and family—Georgia, Joshua, Andrew and Odessa.

My thanks go to all the people who helped me—beginning with Patrick Gallagher, Chairman of Allen & Unwin, who published my last book, *Resilience*, and who was interested, helpful and patient from the beginning to what must have seemed like a never-ending story. Thank you Patrick.

There were two major advisers, without whom I wouldn't have managed: Jackie Yowell, who was on board with my first book, *Tell Me I'm Here*, and ever since has been the voice of wisdom and support; and Christa Munns, Senior Editor at Allen & Unwin, meticulous, patient and brilliant at her work.

Zacha Rosen was there almost from the beginning, helping with research and bringing an ability to find anything that was required or, better still, that would miraculously help. He could also speak harshly to a recalcitrant computer and get it to work.

Diane Harris is one of my oldest friends. She first produced me years ago when I had a daily current affairs program on the Macquarie Network. She always brings relevant and interesting material to light, is enthusiastic, determined and has a special sense of humour. And thanks as always to my ever wise agent, Fiona Inglis.

The most important people of all were, and are, my family and my friends who helped me unlock memories, teased me about ever reaching the finishing line and gave me loving support—perhaps the most needed element in this mysterious process of writing a book.